Reincarnation

and

The Law of Karma

William Walker Atkinson

DD BOOKS
Publishers for New Generations

Reincarnation and the Law of Karma
by William Walker Atkinson

Price: ₹ 250 /-

ISBN: 9789359579702

DD Books
Delhi, India

www.ddbookshub.com
ddsalesglobal@gmail.com

Printed in the **Republic of INDIA**

Reincarnation

and

The Law of Karma

Table of Content

I

The Early Races.

By "Reincarnation" we mean the repeated incarnation, or embodiment in flesh, of the soul or immaterial part of man's nature. The term "Metempsychosis" is frequently employed in the same sense, the definition of the latter term being: "The passage of the soul, as an immortal essence, at the death of the body, into another living body." The term "Transmigration of Souls" is sometimes employed, the term being used in the sense of "passing from one body into another." But the term "Transmigration" is often used in connection with the belief of certain undeveloped races who held that the soul of men sometimes passed into the bodies of the lower animals, as a punishment for their sins committed during the human life. But this belief is held in disrepute by the adherents of Reincarnation or Metempsychosis, and has no connection with their philosophy or beliefs, the ideas having sprung from an entirely different source, and having nothing in common.

There are many forms of belief—many degrees of doctrine—regarding Reincarnation, as we shall see as we proceed, but there is a fundamental and basic principle underlying all of the various shades of opinion, and divisions of the schools. This fundamental belief may be expressed as the doctrine that there is in man an immaterial Something (called the soul, spirit, inner self, or many other names) which does not perish at the death or disintegration of the body, but which persists as an entity, and after a shorter or longer interval of rest reincarnates, or is re-born, into a new body—that of an unborn infant—from whence it proceeds to live a new life in the body, more or less unconscious of its past existences, but containing within itself the "essence" or results of its past lives, which experiences go to make up its new "character," or "personality." It is usually held that the rebirth is governed by the law of attraction, under one name or another, and which law operates in accordance with strict justice, in the direction of attracting the reincarnating soul to a body, and conditions, in accordance with the tendencies of the past life, the parents also attracting to them a soul bound to them by some ties in the past, the law being universal, uniform, and equitable to all concerned in the matter. This is a general statement of the doctrine as it is generally held by the most intelligent of its adherents.

E. D. Walker, a well-known English writer on the subject, gives the following beautiful idea of the general teachings: "Reincarnation teaches that the soul enters this life, not as a fresh creation, but after a long course of previous existences on this earth and elsewhere, in which it acquired its present inhering peculiarities, and that it is on the way to future transformations which the soul is now shaping. It claims that infancy brings to earth, not a blank scroll for the beginning of an earthly record, nor a mere cohesion of atomic forces into a brief personality, soon to dissolve again into the elements, but that it is inscribed with ancestral histories, some like the present scene, most of them unlike it and stretching back into the remotest past. These inscriptions are generally undecipherable, save as revealed in their moulding influence upon the new career; but like the invisible photographic images made by the sun of all it sees, when they are properly developed in the laboratory of consciousness they will be distinctly displayed. The current phase of life will also be stored away in the secret vaults of memory, for its unconscious effects upon the ensuing lives. All the qualities we now possess, in body, mind and soul, result from our use of ancient opportunities. We are indeed 'the heir of all the ages,' and are alone responsible for our inheritances. For these conditions accrue from distant causes engendered by our older selves, and the future flows by the divine law of cause and effect from the gathered momentum of our past impetuses. There is no favoritism in the universe, but all have the same everlasting facilities for growth. Those who are now elevated in worldly station may be sunk in humble surroundings in the future. Only the inner traits of the soul are permanent companions. The wealthy sluggard may be the beggar of the next life; and the industrious worker of the present is sowing the seeds of future greatness. Suffering bravely endured now will produce a treasure of patience and fortitude in another life; hardships will give rise to strength; self-denial must develop the will; tastes cultivated in this existence will somehow bear fruit in coming ones; and acquired energies will assert themselves whenever they can by the Law of Parsimony upon which the principles of physics are based. Vice versa, the unconscious habits, the uncontrollable impulses, the peculiar tendencies, the favorite pursuits, and the soul-stirring friendships of the present descend from far-reaching previous activities."

The doctrine of Reincarnation—Metempsychosis—Rebirth—has always been held as truth by a large portion of the human race. Following the invariable law of cyclic changes—the swing of the pendulum of thought—at times it has apparently died out in parts of the world, only to be again succeeded by a new birth and interest among the descendants of the same people. It is a light impossible to extinguish, and although its flickering flame may seem to die out for a moment, the shifting of the mental winds again allows it to rekindle from the hidden spark, and lo! again it bursts into new life and vigor. The reawakened interest in the subject in the Western world, of which all keen observers have taken note, is but another instance of the operation of the Cyclic Law. It begins to look as if the occultists are right when they predict that before the dawn of another century the Western world will once more have embraced the doctrines of Rebirth—the old, discarded truth, once so dear to the race, will again be settled in popular favor, and again move toward the position of "orthodox" teaching, perhaps to be again crystallized by reason of its "orthodoxy" and again to lose favor and fade away, as the pendulum swings backward to the other extreme of thought.

But the teaching of Reincarnation never has passed away altogether from the race—in some parts of the world the lamp has been kept burning brightly—nay, more, at no time in human history has there been a period in which the majority of the race has not accepted the doctrine of Rebirth, in some of its various forms. It was so one thousand years ago—two thousand—five thousand—and it is so to-day. In this Twentieth Century nearly if not quite two-thirds of the race hold firmly to the teaching, and the multitudes of Hindus and other Eastern peoples cling to it tenaciously. And, even outside of these people, there are to be found traces of the doctrine among other races in the East, and West. So Reincarnation is not a "forgotten truth," or "discarded doctrine," but one fully alive and vigorous, and one which is destined to play a very important part in the history of Western thought during the Twentieth Century.

It is interesting to trace the history of the doctrine among the ancient peoples—away back into the dim recesses of the past. It is difficult to ascribe to any particular time, or any particular race, the credit of having "originated" Reincarnation. In spite of the decided opinions, and the differing theories of the various writers on this subject, who would give Egypt, or India, or the lost Atlantis, as the birthplace of the doctrine, we feel that such ideas are but attempts to attribute a universal intuitive belief to some favored part of the race. We do not believe that the doctrine of Reincarnation ever "originated" anywhere, as a new and distinct doctrine. We believe that it sprang into existence whenever and wherever man arrived at a stage of intellectual development sufficient to enable him to form a mental conception of a Something that lived after Death. No matter from what source this belief in a "ghost" originated, it must be admitted that it is found among all peo ples, and is apparently an universal idea. And, running along with it in the primitive peoples, we find that there is, and always has been, an idea, more or less vague and indistinct, that somehow, someway, sometime, this "ghost" of the person returns to earthly existence and takes upon itself a new fleshly garment—a new body. Here, then, is where the idea of Reincarnation begins—everywhere, at a certain stage of human mental development. It runs parallel with the "ghost" idea, and seems bound up with that conception in nearly every case. When man evolves a little further, he begins to reason that if the "ghost" is immortal, and survives the death of the body, and returns to take upon itself a new body, then it must have lived before the last birth, and therefore must have a long chain of lives behind it. This is the second step. The third step is when man begins to reason that the next life is dependent upon something done or left undone in the present life. And upon these three fundamental ideas the doctrine of Reincarnation has been built. The occultists claim that in addition to this universal idea, which is more or less intuitive, the race has received more or less instruction, from time to time, from certain advanced souls which have passed on to higher planes of existence, and who are now called the Masters, Adepts, Teachers, Race Guides, etc., etc. But whatever may be the explanation, it remains a truth that man seems to have worked out for himself, in all times and in all places, first, an idea of a "ghost" which persists after the body dies; and second, that this "ghost" has lived before in other bodies, and will return again to take on a new body. There are various ideas regarding "heavens" and "hells," but underlying them all there persists this idea of re-birth in some of its phases.

Soldi, the archaeologist, has published an interesting series of works, dealing with the beliefs of primitive peoples, who have passed from the scene of human action. He shows by the fragments of carving and sculpture which have survived them that there was an universal idea among them of the "ghost" which lived after the body died; and a corresponding idea that some day this "ghost" would return to the scene of its former activities. This belief sometimes took the form of a return into the former body, which idea led to the preservation of the body by processes of mummifying, etc., but as a rule this belief developed into the more advanced one of a re-birth in a new body.

The earlier travelers in Africa have reported that here and there they found evidences and traces of what was to them "a strange belief" in the future return of the soul to a new body on earth. The early explorers of America found similar traditions and beliefs among the Red Indians, survivals of which exist even unto this day. It is related of a number of savage tribes, in different parts of the world, that they place the bodies of their dead children by the roadside, in order that their souls may be given a good chance to find new bodies by reason of the approaching of many traveling pregnant women who pass along the road. A number of these primitive people hold to the idea of a complex soul, com posed of several parts, in which they resemble the Egyptians, Hindus, Chinese, and in fact all mystical and occult philosophies. The Figi Islanders are said to believe in a black soul and a white soul, the former of which remains with the buried body and disintegrates with it, while the white soul leaves the body and wanders as a "ghost," and afterward, tiring of the wandering, returns to life in a new body. The natives of Greenland are said to believe in an astral body, which leaves the body during sleep, but which perishes as the body disintegrates after death; and a second soul which leaves the body only at death, and which persists until it is reborn at a later time. In fact, the student finds that nearly all of the primitives races, and those semi-civilized, show traces of a belief in a complex soul, and a trace of doctrine of Reincarnation in some form. The human mind seems to work along the same lines, among the different races—unless one holds to the theory that all sprang from the same root-race, and that the various beliefs are survivals of some ancient fundamental doc trine—the facts are not disturbed in either case.

In the last mentioned connection, we might mention that the traditions concerning Ancient Atlantis—the lost continent—all hold to the effect that her people believed strongly in Reincarnation, and to the ideas of the complex soul. As the survivors of Atlantis are believed to have been the ancestors of the Egyptians on the one hand, and of the Ancient Peruvians on the other—the two branches of survivors having maintained their original doctrines as modified by different environments—we might find here an explanation of the prevalence of the doctrine on both sides of the ocean. We mention this merely in passing, and as of general interest in the line of our subject.

~2~

The Egyptians, Chaldeans, Druids, Etc.

After considering the existence of the doctrines of Reincarnation among the primitive peoples, and its traditional existence among the vanished peoples of the past, we find ourselves irresistibly borne toward that ancient land of mystery—the home of the mystics and occultists of the past—the land of Isis—the home of the builders of the Pyramids—the people of the Sphinx. Whether these people were the direct descendants of the people of destroyed Atlantis, the home of the Ancient Wisdom—or whether they were a new people who had rediscovered the old doctrines—the fact remains that when tracing back any old occult or mystic doctrine we find ourselves gradually led toward the land of the Sphinx as the source of that hidden truth. The Sphinx is a fit emblem of that wonderful race—its sealed lips seem to invite the ultimate questions, and one feels that there may be a whispered answer wafted from those tightly closed lips toward the ear that is prepared to hear and receive it. And so, in our search for the origin of Reincarnation, we find ourselves once more confronting the Egyptian Sphinx as we have done so often before in our search after Truth.

Notwithstanding its obvious prehistoric origin, many have claimed that Metempsychosis has its birthplace in old Egypt, on the banks of the Nile. India disputes this claim, holding that the

Ganges, not the Nile, gave birth to the doctrine. Be that as it may, we shall treat the Egyptian conception at this place, among the ancient lands holding the doctrine, for in India it is not a thing of the past, but a doctrine which has its full flower at the present time, and which flower is sending forth its subtle odor to all parts of the civilized world. And so we shall defer our consideration of India's teachings until we reach the present stage of the history of Reincarnation. Herodotus, many centuries ago, said of the Egyptians that: "The Egyptians are the first who propounded the theory that the human soul is imperishable, and that where the body of any one dies it enters into some other body that may be ready to receive it; and that when it has gone the round of all created forms on land, in water, and in air, then it once more enters the human body born for it; and that this cycle of existence for the soul takes place in three thousand years."

The doctrine of Reincarnation is discernible though hidden away amidst the mass of esoteric doctrine back of the exoteric teachings of the Egyptians, which latter were expounded to the common people, while the truth was reserved for the few who were ready for it. The inner circles of the Egyptian mystics believed in and understood the inner truths of Reincarnation, and although they guarded the esoteric teachings carefully, still fragments fell from the table and were greedily taken up by the masses, as we may see by an examination of the scraps of historical records which have been preserved, graven in the stone, and imprinted on the bricks. Not only did these people accept the doctrine of Reincarnation, but Egypt was really the home of the highest occult teachings. The doctrines and teachings regarding several "sheaths" or "bodies" of man, which are taught by occultists of all times and races, are believed to have been fully taught in their original purity on the banks of the Nile, and in the shadow of the Pyramids—yes, even before the days of the Pyramids. Their forty centuries of history saw many modifications of the philosophical and religious beliefs, but the fundamental doctrine of Reincarnation was held to during the entire period of history in Ancient Egypt, and was not discarded until the decadent descendants of the once mighty race were overwhelmed by stronger races, whose religions and beliefs superseded the vestiges of the Ancient Doctrine. The Egyptians held that there was "Ka," the divine spirit in man; "Ab," the intellect or will; "Hati," the vitality; "Tet," the astral body; "Sahu," the etheric double; and "Xa," the physical body (some authori ties forming a slightly different arrangement), which correspond to the various "bodies of man" as recognized by occultists to-day.

The Ancient Chaldeans also taught the doctrine of Rebirth. The body of Persian and Chaldean mystics and occultists, known as "the Magi," who were masters of the Hidden Wisdom, held to the doctrine of Reincarnation as one of their fundamental truths. In fact, they managed to educate the masses of their people to a much higher point than the masses of the Egyptians, and, escaping the idolatrous tendencies of the Egyptian populace, they manifested a very high degree of pure philosophical, occult, and religious knowledge. The Magi taught that the soul was a complex being, and that certain portions of it perished, while certain other parts survived and passed on through a series of earth and "other-world" existences, until finally it attained such a degree of purity that it was relieved of the necessity for further incarnation, and thenceforth dwelt in the region of ineffable bliss—the region of light eter nal. The teaching also held that just before entering into the state of bliss, the soul was able to review its previous incarnations, seeing distinctly the connection between them, and thus gaining a store of the wisdom of experience, which would aid it in its future work as a helper of future races which would appear on the face of the earth. The

Magi taught that as all living things—nay, all things having existence, organic or inorganic—were but varying manifestations of the One Life and Being, therefore the highest knowledge implied a feeling of conscious brotherhood and relationship toward and with all.

Even among the Chinese there was an esoteric teaching concerning Reincarnation, beneath the outer teaching of ages past. It may be discerned in the teachings of the early philosophers and seers of the race, notably in the work of Lao-Tze, the great Chinese sage and teacher. Lao-Tze, whose great work, the "Tao-Teh-King," is a classic, taught Reincarnation to his inner circle of students and adherents, at least so many authorities claim. He taught that there existed a fundamental principle called "Tao," which is held to have been identical with the "primordial reason," a manifestation of which was the "Teh," or the creative activity of the universe. From the union and action of the "Tao" and the "Teh" proceeded the universe, including the human soul, which he taught was composed of several parts, among them being the "huen," or spiritual principle; and the "phi," or semi-material vital principle, which together animate the body. Lao-Tze said: "To be ignorant that the true self is immortal, is to remain in a grievous state of error, and to experience many calamities by reason thereof. Know ye, that there is a part of man which is subtle and spiritual, and which is the heaven-bound portion of himself; that which has to do with flesh, bones, and body, belongs to the earth; earthly to earth—heavenly to heaven. Such is the Law." Some have held that Lao-Tze taught the immediate return of the "huen" to the "tao" after death, but from the writings of his early followers it may be seen that he really taught that the "huen" persisted in individual existence, throughout repeated incarnations, returning to the "tao" only when it had completed its round of experience-life. For instance, in the Si Haei, it is said that: "The vital essence is dispersed after death together with the body, bones and flesh; but the soul, or knowing principle of the self, is preserved and does not perish. There is no immediate absorption of the individuality into the Tao, for individuality persists, and manifests itself according to the Law." And Chuang-Tze said: "Death is but the commencement of a new life." It was also taught by the early Taoists, that the deeds, good and evil, of the present life would bear fruit in future existences; in addition to the orthodox heavens and hells, in which the Chinese believed, and of which they had a great variety adapted to the requirements of the various grades of saints and sinners, the minute details of which places being described with that attention to minor details and particulars peculiar to the Chinese mind. The teachings of a later date, that the soul of the ancestor abided in the hall of the ancestors, etc., were a corruption of the ancient teaching. Other Chinese teachers taught that the soul consists of three parts, the first being the "kuei," which had its seat in the belly, and which perished with the body; the second being the "ling," which had its seat in the heart or chest, and which persisted for some time after death, but which eventually disintegrated; and the third, or "huen," which had its seat in the brain, and which survived the disintegration of its companions, and then passed on to other existences.

As strange as it may appear to many readers unfamiliar with the subject, the ancient Druids, particularly those dwelling in ancient Gaul, were familiar with the doctrine of Reincarnation, and believed in its tenets. These people, generally regarded as ancient barbarians, really possessed a philosophy of a high order, which merged into a mystic form of religion. Many of the Romans, upon their conquest of Gallia, were surprised at the degree and character of the philosophical knowledge possessed by the Druids, and many of them have left written records of the same, notably in the case of Aristotle, Cæsar,

Lucan, and Valerius Maximus. The Christian teachers who succeeded them also bore witness to these facts, as may be seen by reference to the works of St. Clement, St. Cyril, and other of the early Christian Fathers. These ancient "barbarians" entertained some of the highest spiritual conceptions of life and immortality—the mind and the soul. Reynaud has written of them, basing his statements upon a careful study of the ancient beliefs of this race: "If Judea represents in the world, with a tenacity of its own the idea of a personal and absolute God; if Greece and Rome represent the idea of society, Gaul represents, just as particularly, the idea of immortality. Nothing characterized it better, as all the ancients admit. That mysterious folk was looked upon as the privileged possessor of the secrets of death, and its unwavering instinctive faith in the persistence of life never ceased to be a cause of astonishment, and sometimes of fear, in the eyes of the heathen." The Gauls possessed an occult philosophy, and a mystic religion, which were destroyed by the influences of the Roman Conquest.

The philosophy of the Druids bore a remarkable resemblance to the Inner Doctrine of the Egyptians, and their successors, the Grecian Mystics. Traces of Hermeticism and Pythagoreanism are clearly discernible, although the connecting link that bound them together has been lost to history. Legends among the Druids connected their order with the ancient Aryan creeds and teachings, and there seems to have been a very close connection between these priests and those of Ancient Greece, for there are tales of offerings being sent to the temples of Greece from the priests of Gaul. And it is also related that on the island of Delphos there was once a Druidic tomb in the shape of a monument, believed to have been erected over the remains of Druid priestesses. Herodotus and others speak of a secret alliance between the priests of Greece and those of the Druids. Some of the ancient legends hold that Pythagoras was the instructor of the Druidic priests, and that Pythagoras himself was in close communication with the Brahmins of India, and the Hermetists of Egypt. Other legends have it that the Druids received their first instruction from Zamolais, who had been a slave and student of Pythagoras. At any rate, the correspondence between the two schools of philosophy is remarkable.

Much of the Druidic teachings has been lost, and it is difficult to piece together the fragments. But enough is known to indicate the above mentioned relationship to the Pythagorean school, and of the firm hold of the doctrine of Reincarnation upon the Druids. The preserved fragments show that the Druids taught that there was in man an immaterial, spiritual part, called "Awen," which proceeded from an Universal Spiritual Principle of Life. They taught that this "Awen" had animated the lower forms of life, mineral, vegetable and animal, before incarnating as man. In those conditions it was entangled and im prisoned in the state of "abysmal circling," called "Anufu," from which it finally escaped and entered into the "circle of freedom," called "Abred," or human incarnation and beyond. This state of "Abred" includes life in the various human races on this and other planets, until finally there is a further liberation of the "Awen," which then passes on to the "Circle of Bliss," or "Gwynfid," where it abides for æons in a state of ecstatic being. But, beyond even this transcendent state, there is another, which is called the "Circle of the Infinite," or "Ceugant," which is identical with the "Union with God" of the Persians and Greek Mystics, or the "Nirvana" of the Hindus. Rather an advanced form of philosophy for "barbarians," is it not? Particularly when contrasted with the crude mythology of the Roman conquerors!

The Gauls were so advanced in the practical phases of occultism that they gave every condemned criminal a respite of five years, after sentence of death, before execution, in order that he might prepare him self for a future state by meditation, instruction and other preparation; and also to prevent ushering an unprepared and guilty soul into the plane of the departed—the advantages of which plan is apparent to every student of occultism who accepts the teaching regarding the astral planes.

The reader will understand, of course, that the degree of advancement in spiritual and philosophical matters evidenced by the Gauls was due not to the fact that these people were generally so far advanced beyond their neighbors, but rather to the fact that they had been instructed by the Druid priests among them. Tradition has it that the original Druidic priests came to Gaul and other countries from some far-off land, probably from Egypt or Greece. We have spoken of the connection between their teachings and that of the Pythagoreans, and there was undoubtedly a strong bond of relationship between these priests and the occultists of other lands. The Druidic priests were well versed in astronomy and astrology, and the planets had an important part in the teachings. A portion of their ritual is said to have correspondences with the early Jewish rites and worship. Their favorite symbol—the mistletoe—was used as indicating re-birth, the mistletoe being the new life springing forth from the old one, typified by the oak. The Druids traveled into Ancient Britain and Ireland, and many traces of their religious rites may still be found there, not only in the shape of the stone places-of-worship, but also in many curious local customs among the peasantry. Many a bit of English folk-lore—many an odd Irish fancy concerning fairies and the like; symbols of good-luck; banshees and "the little-folk"—came honestly to these people from the days of the Druids. And from the same source came the many whispered tales among both races regarding the birth of children who seemed to have remembrances of former lives on earth, which memory faded away as they grew older. Among these people there is always an undercurrent of mystic ideas about souls "coming back" in some mysterious way not fully understood. It is the inheritance from the Druids.

~3~

The Romans and Greeks.

One unfamiliar with the subject would naturally expect to find the Ancient Romans well advanced along the lines of philosophy, religion, and spiritual speculation, judging from the all-powerful influence exerted by them over the affairs of the whole known world. Particularly when one considers the relationship with and connection of Rome with ancient Greece, it would seem that the two peoples must have had much in common in the world of thought. But such is not the case. Although the exoteric religions of the Romans resembled that of the Greeks, from whom it was borrowed or inherited, there was little or no original thought along metaphysics, religion or philosophy among the Romans. This was probably due to the fact that the whole tendency of Rome was toward material ad vancement and attainment, little or no attention being given to matters concerning the soul, future life, etc. Some few of the philosophers of Rome advanced theories regarding the future state, but beyond a vague sort of ancestor worship the masses of the people took but little interest in the subject. Cicero, it is true, uttered words which indicate a belief in immortality, when he said in "Scipio's Dream": "Know that it is not thou, but thy body alone, which is mortal. The individual in his entirety resides in the soul, and not in the outward form. Learn, then, that thou art a god; thou, the immortal intelligence which gives movements to a perishable body, just as the eternal God animates an incorruptible body." Pliny the younger left writings which seem to indicate his belief in the reality of phantoms, and Ovid has written verses which would indicate his recognition of a part of man which survived the death of the body. But, on the whole, Roman philosophy treated immortality as a thing perchance existing, but not proven, and to be viewed rather as a poetical ex pression of a longing, rather than as an established, or at least a well grounded, principle of philosophical thought. But Lucretius and others of his time and country protested against the folly of belief in the survival of the soul held by the other nations. He said that: "The fear of eternal life should be banished from the universe; it disturbs the peace of mankind, for it prevents the enjoyment of any security or pleasure." And Virgil praised and commended the philosophical attitude which was able to see the real cause of things, and was therefore able to reject the unworthy fear of a world beyond and all fears arising from such belief. But even many of the Roman philosophers, while denying immortality, believed in supernatural powers and beings, and were very superstitious and childlike in many respects, so that their philosophy of non-survival was evidently rather the result of temperament and pursuit of material things than a height of philosophical reasoning or metaphysical thought.

And so, the Romans stand apart from the majority of the ancient peoples, in so far as the belief in Reincarnation is concerned. While there were individual mystics and occultists among them, it still remains a fact that the majority of the people held no such belief, and in fact the masses had no clearly defined ideas regarding the survival of the soul. It is a strange exception to the general rule, and one that has occasioned much comment and attention among thinkers along these lines. There was a vague form of ancestor worship among the Romans, but even this was along the lines of collective survival of the ancestors, and was free from the ordinary metaphysical speculations and religious dogmas. Roughly stated, the Roman belief may be expressed by an idea of a less material, or more subtle, part of man which escaped disintegration after death, and which in some mysterious way passed on to combine with the ancestral soul which composed the collective ancestral deity of the family, the peace and pleasure of which were held as sacred duties on the part of the descendants, sacri fices and offerings being made toward this end. Nevertheless, here and there, among the Romans, were eminent thinkers who seemingly held a vague, tentative belief in some form of Reincarnation, as, for instance, Ovid, who says: "Nothing perishes, although everything changes here on earth; the souls come and go unendingly in visible forms; the animals which have acquired goodness will take upon them human form"; and Virgil says: "After death, the souls come to the Elysian fields, or to Tartarus, and there meet with the reward or punishment of their deeds during life. Later, on drinking of the waters of Lethe, which takes away all memory of the past, they return to earth." But it must be admitted that Rome was deficient in spiritual insight and beliefs, on the whole, her material successes having diverted her attention from the problems which had so engrossed the mind of her neighbor Greece, and her older sisters Persia, Chaldea, and Egypt.

Among the Greeks, on the contrary, we find a marked degree of interest and spec ulation regarding the immortality of the soul, and much interest in the doctrines of Metempsychosis or Reincarnation. Although the great masses of the Grecian people were satisfied with their popular mythology and not disposed to question further, or to indulge in keen speculation on metaphysical subjects, still the intellectual portion of the race were most active in their search after truth, and their schools of philosophy, with their many followers and adherents, have left an indelible mark upon the thought of man unto this day. Next to the Hindus, the Greeks were the great philosophers of the human race. And the occultists and mystics among them were equal to those of Persia, India, Chaldea or Egypt. While the various theories regarding the soul were as the sands of the sea, so many were the teachers, schools and divisions of thought among these people—still the doctrine of Reincarnation played a very important part in their philosophy. The prevailing idea was that the worthy souls pass on to a state of bliss, without rebirth, while the less worthy pass the waters of the river of Lethe, quaffing of its waters of forgetfulness, and thus having the recollection of their earth-life, and of the period of punishment that they had undergone by reason of the same, obliterated and cleansed from their memories, when they pass on to re-birth. One of the old Orphic hymns reads as follows: "The wise love light and not darkness. When you travel the journey of Life, remember, always, the end of the journey. When souls return to the light, after their sojourn on earth, they wear upon their more subtle bodies, like searing, hideous scars, the marks of their earthly sins—these must be obliterated, and they go back to earth to be cleansed. But the pure, virtuous and strong proceed direct to the Sun of Dionysus." The teachings of the Egyptians left a deep impression upon the Grecian mind, and not only the common form of belief, but also the esoteric doctrines, were passed along to the newer people by the elder.

Pythagoras was the great occult teacher of Greece, and his school and that of his followers accepted and taught the great doctrine of Reincarnation. Much of his teaching was reserved for the initiates of the mystic orders founded by himself and his followers, but still much of the doctrine was made public. Both Orpheus and Pythagoras, although several centuries separated them, were students at the fount of knowledge in Egypt, having traveled to that country in order to be initiated in the mystic orders of the ancient land, and returning they taught anew the old doctrine of Rebirth. The Pythagorean teaching resembles that of the Hindus and Egyptians, in so far as is concerned the nature of man—his several bodies or sheaths—and the survival of the higher part of his nature, while the lower part perishes. It was taught that after death this higher part of the soul passed on to a region of bliss, where it received knowledge and felt the beneficent influence of developed and advanced souls, thus becoming equipped for a new life, with incentives toward higher things. But, not having as yet reached the stage of development which will entitle it to dwell in the blissful regions for all eternity, it sooner or later reaches the limit of its term of probation, and then passes down toward another incarnation on earth—another step on the Path of Attainment.

The teaching was, further, that the conditions, circumstances and environments of the new earth-life were determined by the actions, thoughts, and mental tendencies of the former life, and by the degree of development which the several previous earth-lives had manifested. In this respect the teaching agrees materially with the universal doctrine regarding Reincarnation and Karma. Pythagoras taught that the doctrine of Reincarnation accounted for the inequality observable in the lives of men on earth, giving a logical reason for the same, and establishing the fact of universal and ultimate justice, accountable for on no other grounds. He taught that although the material world was subject to the laws of destiny and fatality, yet there was another and higher state of being in which the soul would rise above the laws of the lower world. This higher state, he taught, had laws of its own, as yet unknown to man, which tended to work out the imperfect laws of the material world, establishing harmony, justice, and equality, to supply the apparent deficiencies manifested in the earth life.

Following Pythagoras, Plato, the great Grecian philosopher, taught the old-new doctrine of Rebirth. He taught that the souls of the dead must return to earth, where, in new lives, they must wear out the old earth deeds, receiving benefits for the worthy ones, and penalties for the unworthy ones, the soul profiting by these repeated experiences, and rising step by step toward the divine. Plato taught that the reincarnated soul has flashes of remembrance of its former lives, and also instincts and intuitions gained by former experiences. He classed innate ideas among these inherited experiences of former lives. It has been well said that "everything can be found in Plato," and therefore one who seeks for the ancient Grecian ideas concerning Reincarnation, and the problems of the soul, may find that which he seeks in the writings of the old sage and philosopher. Plato was the past master of the inner teachings concerning the soul, and all who have followed him have drawn freely from his great store of wisdom. His influence on the early Christian church was enormous, and in many forms it continues even unto this day. Many of the early Christian fathers taught that Plato was really one of the many forerunners of Christ, who had prepared the pagan world for the coming of the Master.

In "Phaedo," Plato describes the soul, and explains its immortality. He teaches that man has a material body which is subject to constant change, and subject to death and disintegration; and also an immaterial soul, unchangeable and indestructible, and akin to the divine. At death this soul was severed from its physical companion, and rose, purified, to the higher regions, where it rendered an account of itself, and had its future allotted to it. If it was found sufficiently untainted and unsullied by the mire of material life, it was considered fit to be admitted to the State of Bliss, which was described as Union with the Supreme Being, which latter is described as Spirit, eternal and omniscient. The base and very guilty souls undergo a period of punishment, or purgation, to the end that they may be purged and purified of the guilt, before being allowed to make another trial for perfection. The souls which were not sufficiently pure for the State of Bliss, nor yet so impure that they need the purging process, were returned to earth-life, there to take up new bodies, and endeavor to work out their salvation anew, to the end that they might in the future attain the Blissful State. Plato taught that in the Rebirth, the soul was generally unconscious of its previous lives, although it may have flashes of recollection. Besides this it has a form of intuition, and innate ideas, which was believed to be the result of the experiences gained in the past lives, and which knowledge had been stored up so as to benefit the soul in its reincarnated existence.

Plato taught that the immaterial part of man—the soul—was a complex thing, being composed of a number of differing, though related, elements. Highest in the hierarchy of the soul elements he placed the Spirit, which, he taught, comprised consciousness, intelligence, will, choice between good and evil, etc., and which was absolutely indestructible and immortal, and which had its seat in the head. Then came two other parts of the soul, which survived the dissolution of the body, but which were only comparatively immortal, that is, they were subject to later dissolution and disintegration. Of these semi-material elements, one was the seat of the affections, passions, etc., and was located in the heart; while the other, which was the seat of the sensual and lower desires, passions, etc., was located in the liver. These two mentioned lower elements were regarded as not possessed of reason, but still having certain powers of sensation, perception, and will.

The Neo-Platonists, who followed Plato, and who adapted his teachings to their many conflicting ideas, held firmly to the doctrine of Reincarnation. The writings of Plotinus, Porphyry, and the other Mystics, had much to say on this subject, and the teaching was much refined under their influence. The Jewish philosophers were affected by the influence of the Platonic thought, and the school of the Essenes, which held firmly to the idea of Rebirth, was a source from which Christianity received much of its early influence.

~4~

The Jews, Essenes and Early Christians.

The early Jewish people had an Inner Teaching which embraced certain ideas concerning Reincarnation, although the masses of the people knew nothing of the doctrine which was reserved for the inner circles of the few. There is much dispute concerning the early beliefs of the Jewish people regarding the immortality of the soul. The best authorities seem to agree that the early beliefs were very crude and indefinite, consisting principally of a general belief that after death the souls are gathered up together in a dark place, called Sheol, where they dwell in an unconscious sleep. It will be noted that the earlier books in the Old Testament have very little to say on this subject. Gradually, however, there may be noticed a dawning belief in certain states of the departed souls, and in this the Jews were undoubtedly influenced by the conceptions of the people of other lands with whom they came in contact. The sojourn in Egypt must have exerted an important influence on them, particularly the educated thinkers of the race, of which, however, there were but few, owing to the condition in which they were kept as bondsmen of the Egyptians. Moses, however, owing to his education and training among the Egyptian priests, must have been fully initiated in the Mysteries of that land, and the Jewish legends would indicate that he formed an Inner Circle of the priesthood of his people, after they escaped from Egypt, and doubtless instructed them fully in the occult doctrines, which, however, were too advanced and complicated for preaching to the mass of ignorant people of which the Jewish race of that time was composed. The lamp of learning among the Jews of that time was kept alight but by very few priests among them. There has always been much talk, and legend, concerning this Inner Teaching among the Jews. The Jewish Rabbis have had so much to say regarding it, and some of the Early Fathers of the Christian Church were of the opinion that such Secret Doctrine existed.

Scholars have noted that in important passages in the Jewish Bible, three distinct terms are used in referring to the immaterial part, or "soul," of man. These terms are "Nichema," "Rouach," and "Nephesh," respectively, and have been translated as "soul," "spirit" or "breath," in several senses of these terms. Many good authorities have held that these three terms did not apply to one conception, but that on the contrary they referred to three distinct elements of the soul, akin to the conceptions of the Egyptians and other early peoples, who held to the trinity of the soul, as we have shown a little further back. Some Hebrew scholars hold that "Nichema" is the Ego, or Intelligent Spirit; "Rouach," the lower vehicle of the Ego; and "Nephesh," the Vital Force, Vitality, or Life.

Students of the Kaballah, or Secret Writings of the Jews, find therein many references to the complex nature of the soul, and its future states, as well as undoubted teachings regarding Reincarnation, or Future Existence in the Body. The Kaballah was the book of the Jewish Mysteries, and was largely symbolical, so that to those unacquainted with the symbols employed, it read as if lacking sense or meaning. But those having the key, were able to read therefrom many bits of hidden doctrine. The Kaballah is said to be veiled in seven coverings—that is, its symbology is sevenfold, so that none but those having the inner keys may know the full truth contained therein, although even the first key will unlock many doors. The Zohar, another Secret Book of the Jews, although of much later origin than the Kaballah, also contains much of the Inner Teachings concerning the destiny of the soul. This book plainly recognizes and states the three-fold nature of the soul, above mentioned, and treats the Nichema, Rouach and Nephesh as distinct elements thereof. It also teaches that when the soul leaves the body it goes through a long and tedious purifying process, whereby the effect of its vices is worn off by means of a series of transmigrations and reincarnations, wherein it develops several perfections, etc. This idea of attaining perfection through repeated rebirths, instead of the rebirths being in the nature of punishment as taught by Plato, is also taught in the Kaballah, showing the agreement of the Jewish mind on this detail of the doctrine. The essence of the Kaballic teaching on this subject is that the souls undergo repeated rebirth, after long intervals of rest and purification, in entire forgetfulness of their previous existences, and for the purpose of advancement, unfoldment, purification, development, and attainment. The Zohar follows up this teaching strictly, although with amplifications. The following quotation from the Zohar is interesting, inasmuch as it shows the teaching on the subject in a few words. It reads as follows: "All souls are subject to the trials of transmigration; and men do not know which are the ways of the Most High in their regard. They do not know how many transformations and mysterious trials they must undergo; how many souls and spirits come to this world without returning to the palace of the divine king. The souls must re-enter the absolute substance whence they have emerged. But to accomplish this end they must develop all the perfections; the germ of which is planted in them; and if they have not fulfilled this condition during one life, they must commence another, a third, and so on, until they have acquired the condition which fits them for reunion with God."

The mystic sect which sprung up among the Jewish people during the century preceding the birth of Christ, and which was in the height of its influence at the time of the Birth—the sect, cult, or order of The Essenes—was an important influence in the direction of spreading the truths of Reincarnation among the Jewish people. This order combined the earlier Egyptian Mysteries with the Mystic Doctrine of Pythagoras and the philosophy of Plato. It was closely connected with the Jewish Therapeutæ of Egypt, and was the leading mystic order of the time. Josephus, the eminent Jewish historian, writing of the Essenes, says: "The opinion obtains among them that bodies indeed are corrupted, and the matter of them not permanent, but that souls continue exempt from death forever; and that emanating from the most subtle ether they are unfolded in bodies as prisons to which they are drawn by some natural spell. But when loosed from the bonds of flesh, as if released from a long captivity, they rejoice and are borne upward." In the New International Encyclopedia (vol. vii, page 217) will be found an instructive article on "Essenes," in which it is stated that among the Essenes there was a certain "view entertained regarding the origin, present state, and future destiny of the soul, which was held to be pre-existent, being entrapped in the body as a prison," etc. And in the same article the following statement occurs: "It is an interesting question as to how much Christianity owes to Essenism. It would seem that there was room for definite contact between John the Baptist and this Brotherhood. His time of preparation was spent in the wilderness near the Dead Sea; his preaching of righteousness toward God, and justice toward one's fellow men, was in agreement with Essenism; while his insistence upon Baptism was in accordance with the Essenic emphasis on lustrations." In this very conservative statement is shown the intimate connection between the Essenes and Early Christianity, through John the Baptist. Some hold that Jesus had a still closer relationship to the Essenes and allied mystic orders, but we shall not insist upon this point, as it lies outside of the ordinary channels of historical information. There is no doubt, however, that the Essenes, who had such a strong influence on the early Christian Church, were closely allied to other mystic organizations with whom they agreed in fundamental doctrines, notably that of Reincarnation. And so we have brought the story down to the early Christian Church, at which point we will continue it. We have left the phase of the subject which pertains to India for separate consideration, for in India the doctrine has had its principal home in all ages, and the subject in that phase requires special treatment.

That there was an Inner Doctrine in the early Christian Church seems to be well established, and that a part of that doctrine consisted in a teaching of Pre-existence of the Soul and some form of Rebirth or Reincarnation seems quite reasonable to those who have made a study of the subject. There is a constant reference to the "Mysteries" and "Inner Teachings" throughout the Epistles, particularly those of Paul, and the writings of the Early Christian Fathers are filled with references to the Secret Doctrines. In the earlier centuries of the Christian Era frequent references are found to have been made to "The Mysteries of Jesus," and that there was an Inner Circle of advanced Christians devoted to mysticism and little known doctrines there can be no doubt. Celsus attacked the early church, alleging that it was a secret organization which taught the Truth to the select few, while it passed on to the multitude only the crumbs of half-truth, and popular teachings veiling the Truth. Origen, a pupil of St. Clement, answered Celsus, stating that while it was true that there were Inner Teachings in the Christian Church, that were not revealed to the populace, still the Church in following that practice was but adhering to the established custom of all philosophies and religions, which gave the esoteric truths only to those who were ready to receive them, at the same time giving to the general mass of followers the exoteric or outer teachings, which were all they could understand or assimilate. Among other things, in this reply, Origen says: "That there should be certain doctrines, not made known to the multitude, which are divulged after the exoteric ones have been taught, is not a peculiarity of Christianity alone, but also of philosophic systems in which certain truths are exoteric and others esoteric. Some of the followers of Pythagoras were content with his 'ipse dixit,' while others were taught in secret those doctrines which were not deemed fit to be communicated to profane and insufficiently prepared ears. Moreover, all the mysteries that are celebrated everywhere through Greece and barbarous countries, although held in secret, have no discredit thrown upon them, so that it is in vain he endeavors to calumniate the secret doctrines of Christianity, seeing that he does not correctly understand its nature." In this quotation it will be noticed that not only does Origen positively admit the existence of the Inner Teachings, but that he also mentions Pythagoras and his school, and also the other Mysteries of Greece, showing his acquaintance with them, and his comparison of them with the Christian Mysteries, which latter he would not have been likely to have done were their teachings repugnant to, and at utter variance with, those of his own church. In the same writing Origen says: "But on these subjects much, and that of a mystical kind, might be said, in keeping with which is the following: 'It is good to keep close to the secret of a king,' in order that the entrance of souls into bodies may not be thrown before the common understanding." Scores of like quotations might be cited.

The writings of the Early Fathers of the Christian Church are filled with many allusions to the current inner doctrine of the pre-existence and rebirth of souls. Origen in particular has written at great length regarding these things. John the Baptist was generally accepted as the reincarnation of Elias, even by the populace, who regarded it as a miraculous occurrence, while the elect regarded it as merely another instance of rebirth under the law. The Gnostics, a mystic order and school in the early church, taught Reincarnation plainly and openly, bringing upon themselves much persecution at the hands of the more conservative. Others held to some form of the teaching, the disputes among them being principally regarding points of doctrine and detail, the main teachings being admitted. Origen taught that souls had fallen from a high estate and were working their way back toward their lost estate and glory, by means of repeated incarnations. Justin Martyr speaks of the soul inhabiting successive bodies, with loss of memory of past lives. For several centuries the early Church held within its bosom many earnest advocates of Reincarnation, and the teaching was recognized as vital even by those who combatted it.

Lactinus, at the end of the third century, held that the idea of the soul's immortality implied its pre-existence. St. Augustine, in his "Confessions," makes use of these remarkable words: "Did I not live in another body before entering my mother's womb?" Which expression is all the more remarkable because Augustine opposed Origen in many points of doctrine, and because it was written as late as A. D. 415. The various Church Councils, however, frowned upon these outcroppings of the doctrine of Reincarnation, and the influence of those who rose to power in the church was directed against the "heresy." At several councils were the teachings rebuked, and condemned, until finally in A. D. 538, Justinian had a law passed which declared that: "Whoever shall support the mythical presentation of the pre-existence of the soul and the consequently wonderful opinion of its return, let him be Anathema." Speaking of the Jewish

Kaballists, an authority states: "Like Origen and other church Fathers, the Kaballists used as their main argument in favor of the doctrine of metempsychosis, the justice of God."

But the doctrine of Reincarnation among Christian races did not die at the orders and commands of the Christian Church Councils. Smouldering under the blanket of opposition and persecution, it kept alive until once more it could lift its flame toward Heaven. And even during its suppression the careful student may see little flickers of the flame—little wreathings of smoke—escaping here and there. Veiled in mystic phrasing, and trimmed with poetic figure, many allusions may be seen among the writings of the centuries. And during the past two hundred years the revival in the subject has been constant, until at the close of the Nineteenth Century, and the begin ning of the Twentieth Century, we once more find the doctrine openly preached and taught to thousands of eager listeners and secretly held even by many orthodox Christians.

☯☯☯

~5~

The Hindus.

While Reincarnation has been believed and taught in nearly every nation, and among all races, in former or present times, still we are justified in considering India as the natural Mother of the doctrine, inasmuch as it has found an especially favorable spiritual and mental environment in that land and among its people, the date of its birth there being lost in the cloudiness of ancient history, but the tree of the teaching being still in full flower and still bearing an abundance of fruit. As the Hindus proudly claim, while the present dominant race was still in the savage, cave-dwelling, stone-age stage of existence—and while even the ancient Jewish people were beginning to place the foundation stones of their religion, of which the present Christian religion is but an offshoot—the great Hindu religious teachers and philosophers had long since firmly established their philosophies and religions with the doctrine of Reincarnation and its accompanying teachings, which had been accepted as Truth by the great Aryan race in India. And, throughout forty centuries, or more, this race has held steadfastly to the original doctrine, until now the West is looking again to it for light on the great problems of human life and existence, and now, in the Twentieth Century, many careful thinkers consider that in the study and understanding of the great fundamental thoughts of the Vedas and the Upanishads, the West will find the only possible antidote to the virus of Materialism that is poisoning the veins of Western spiritual understanding.

The idea of reincarnation is to be found in nearly all of the philosophies and religions of the race, at least in some period in their history—among all peoples and races—yet, in India do we find the doctrine in the fullest flower, not only in the past but in the present. From the earliest ages of the race in India, Reincarnation in some of its various forms has been the accepted doctrine, and today it is accepted by the entire Hindu people, with their many divisions and sub-races, with the exception of the Hindu Mohammedans. The teeming millions of India live and die in the full belief in Reincarnation, and to them it is accepted without a question as the only rational doctrine concerning the past, present and future of the soul. Nowhere on this planet is there to be found such an adherence to the idea of "soul" life—the thinking Hindu always regarding himself as a soul occupying a body, rather than as a body "having a soul," as so many of the Western people seem to regard themselves. And, to the Hindus, the present life is truly regarded as but one step on the stairway of life, and not as the only material life preceding an eternity of spiritual existence. To the Hindu mind, Eternity is here with us Now—we are in eternity as much this moment as we ever shall be—and the present life is but one of a number of fleeting moments in the eternal life.

The early Hindus did not possess the complicated forms of religion now existing among them, with their various creeds, ceremonials, rituals, cults, schools, and denominations. On the contrary, their original form of religion was an advanced form of what some have called "Nature-Worship," but which was rather more than that which the Western mind usually means by the term. Their "Nature" was rather a "Spirit of Nature," or One Life, of which all existing forms are but varying manifestations. Even in this early stage of their religious development they held to a belief in reincarnation of the soul, from one form to another. While to them everything was but a manifestation of One Life, still the soul was a differentiated unit, emanated from the One Life, and destined to work its way back to Unity and Oneness with the Divine Life through many and varied incarnations, until finally it would be again merged with the One. From this early beginning arose the many and varied forms of religious philosophy known to the India of today; but clinging to all these modern forms is to be found the fundamental basis idea of reincarnation and final absorption with the One.

Brahmanism came first, starting from the simple and working to the complex, a great priesthood gradually arising and surrounding the original simple religious philosophy with ceremonial, ritual and theological and metaphysical abstractions and speculation. Then arose Buddhism, which, in a measure, was a return to the primitive idea, but which in turn developed a new priesthood and religious organization. But the fundamental doctrine of Reincarnation permeated them all, and may be regarded as the great common centre of the Hindu religious thought and philosophy.

The Hindu religious books are filled with references to the doctrine of Reincarnation. The Laws of Manu, one of the oldest existing pieces of Sanscrit writing, contains many mentions of it, and the Upanishads and Vedas contain countless reference to it. In the Bhagavad Gita, Krishna says to Arjuna: "Know thou, O Prince of Pandu, that there never was a time when I, nor thou, nor any of these princes of earth was not; nor shall there ever come a time, hereafter, when any of us shall cease to be. As the soul, wearing this material body, experienceth the stages of infancy, youth, manhood, and old age, even so shall it, in due time, pass on to another body, and in other incarnations shall it again live, and move and play its part. * * * These bodies, which act as enveloping coverings for the souls occupying them, are but finite things—things of the moment—and not the Real Man at all. They perish as all finite things perish—let them perish. He who in his ignorance thinketh: 'I slay' or 'I am slain,' babbleth like an infant lacking knowledge. Of a truth none can slay—none can be slain. Take unto thy inner mind this truth, O Prince! Verily, the Real Man—the Spirit of Man—is neither born, nor doth it die. Unborn, undying, ancient, perpetual and eternal, it hath endured, and will endure forever. The body may die; be slain; be destroyed completely—but he that hath occupied it remaineth unharmed. * * * As a man throweth away his old garments, replacing them with new and brighter ones, even so the Dweller of the body, having quitted its old mortal frame, entereth into others which are new and freshly prepared for it. * * * Many have been my births and rebirths, O Prince—and many also have been thine own. But between us lies this difference—I am conscious of all my many lives, but thou lackest remembrance of thine."

In the Mahabarata is said: "Even as when he casteth off an old garment, man clothes himself in new raiment, even so the soul, casting off the wornout body, takes on a new body, avoids the fatal paths leading to hell, works for its salvation, and proceeds toward heaven."

The Brhadaranyakopanishad, one of the old Hindu writings, contains the following: "As the caterpillar, getting to the end of the straw, takes itself away after finding a resting place in advance, so the soul leaving this body, and finding another place in advance, takes himself off from his original abode. As the goldsmith taking little by little of the gold expands it into a new form, so, indeed, does this soul, leaving this body, make a new and happy abode for himself."

But to attempt to quote passages relating to incarnation from the Hindu books, would be akin to compiling a library of many volumes. The sacred writings of the East are filled with references to Reincarnation, and if the latter were eliminated it would be "like the play of Hamlet with Hamlet omitted."

We cannot enter into a description of the various schools of Hindu religious thought and philosophy in this work, for to do so would be to expand this little volume in several of larger size, so extended is the subject. But underlying the many divisions and subdivisions of Hindu thought may be found the fundamental idea of an original emanation from, or manifestation of, One Divine Being, Power and Energy, into countless differentiated units, atoms, or egos, which units, embodying in matter, are unconscious of the spirit ual nature, and take on a consciousness corresponding with the form in which they are embodied. Then follows a series of embodiments, or incarnations, from lower to higher, in which occurs an evolution or "unfoldment" of the nature of the soul, in which it rises to higher and higher planes of being, until finally, after æons of time, it enters in Union with the Divine Nirvana and Para-Nirvana—the state of Eternal Bliss.

The great difference between the Hindu thought and the Grecian is that while the Greeks considered repeated life with joy as a means of greater and greater expression of life, the Hindus, on the contrary, regard life as but a period of travail and sorrow, the only light to be perceived being the expectation and hope of eventually emerging from the region of materiality, and illusion, and regaining true existence in the Spirit. The Hindus nearly all agree that this material life is occasioned by "avidya" or ignorance on the part of the soul of its own real nature and being, whereby it fails to recognize that this ma terial life is "maya" or illusion. They hold that Wisdom consists in the soul recognizing its real nature, and perceiving the illusion of material life and things, and striving to liberate itself from the bondage of materiality and ignorance.

The principal differences among the various Hindu schools of religion and philosophical thought arise from their differing views regarding the nature and constitution of the soul on the one hand, and the means of attaining liberation and freedom from material embodiment on the other. The doctrine of "Karma" of spiritual cause and effect, which we shall consider in another chapter, also runs along with all the varying Hindu conceptions, doctrines, and theories.

Without considering the matter of differences of opinion between the various schools, concerning the nature and constitution of the soul, we may say that all the schools practically agree that the constitution of Man is a complex thing, comprising a number of sheaths, bodies, coverings, or elements, from the grosser to the more spiritual, the various sheaths being discarded as the soul advances on its way toward perfection. There are disputes between the various schools regarding terminology and the precise arrangement of these "principles," but the following classification will answer for the purpose of giving a general idea of the Hindu views on the subject, subject always to the conflicting claims of the various schools. The classification is as follows, passing from lower to higher:

1. Physical or material body, or Rupa. 2. Vitality of Vital Force, or Prana-Jiva. 3. Astral Body, Etheric Double, or Linga Sharira. 4. Animal Soul, or Kama Rupa. 5. Human Soul, or Manas. 6. Spiritual Soul, or Buddhi. 7. Divine Spirit, or Atma.

From the beginning, the tendency of the Hindu mind was in the direction of resolving the universe of forms, shapes, and change, back into some One Underlying Principle, from which all the phenomenal world emerged—some One Infinite Energy, from which all else emerged, emanated, or evolved. And the early Hindu mind busied itself actively with the solution of the problem of this One Being manifesting a Becoming into Many. Just as is the Western world of today actively engaged in solving many material problems, so was ancient India active in solving many spiritual problems—just as the modern West is straining every energy toward discovering the "How," so was ancient India straining every effort to discovering the "Why." And from that struggle of the mind of India there arose countless schools of religious and philosophical thought, many of which have passed away, but many of which persist today. The problem of the relationship of the human soul to the One Being, and the secondary problem of the life, present and future, of the individual soul, is a most vital one to all thinking Hindus today as in the forty centuries or more of its philosophical history. To the Hindu mind, all material research is of minor importance, the important Truth being to discover that "which when once known, all else is understood." But, as we have said, in spite of the numerous religions, schools, and phases of teaching, among the Hindus, the one fundamental conception of Reincarnation is never lost sight of, nor is it ever doubted in any of the forms of the philosophies or religions.

Ignoring the subdivisions of Hindu philosophical thought, we may say that the Hindu philosophies may be divided into a few general classes, several of which we shall now hastily consider, that you may get a glimpse at the variety of Hindu speculative philosophy in its relation to the soul and its destiny. You will, of course, understand that we can do no more than mention the leading features of each class, as a careful consideration would require volumes for each particular school.

We will first consider the philosophy of Kanada, generally known as the Vaisheshika Teaching, which inclines toward an Atomic Theory, akin to that formulated by the old Greek philosopher Democritus. According to this teaching the substance of the universe is composed of an infinite number of atoms, which are eternal, and which were not created by God, but which are co-eternal with Him. These atoms, combining and forming shapes, forms, etc., are the basis of the material universe. It is held, however, that the power or energy whereby these atoms combine and thus form matter, comes from God. This teaching holds that God is a Personal Being, possessing Omnipotence, Omniscience, and Omnipresence. It is also held that there are two substances, or principles, higher, that the material energies or substance, namely, Manas, or Mind, and Atman, or Spirit. Manas or Mind is held to be something like a Mind-Stuff, from which all individual minds are built up—and which Mind-Stuff is held to be eternal. Atman, or Spirit, is held to be an eternal principle, from which the Selves or Souls are differentiated. The Atman, or Spirit, or Self, is regarded as much higher than Mind, which is its tool and instrument of expression. This philosophy teaches that through progression, by Reincarnation, the soul advances from lower to higher states, on its road to freedom and perfection.

Another great school of Hindu philosophy is the philosophy of Kapila, generally known as the Sankhya system. This teaching opposes the Atomic Theory of the Vaisheshika system, and holds that the atoms are not indestructible nor eternal, but may be resolved back into a primal substance called Prakriti. Prakriti is held to be an universal, eternal energy or ethereal substance, something similar to certain Western scientific conceptions of an Universal Ether. From this eternal, universal energy, Kapila held that all the universe has been evolved—all material forms or manifestations of energy being but manifestations of Prakriti. But, the Sankhya system is not materialistic, as might be supposed at first glance, for side by side with Prakriti it offers the principle of Purusha, or Soul, or Spirit, of which all individual souls are atomic units—the Principle of Purusha being an Unity of Units, and not an Undivided One. The Purusha—that is, its units or Individual Souls—is regarded as eternal and immortal. Prakriti is devoid of mind, but is pos sessed of active vital energy, and is capable of producing forms and material manifestations by reason of its inherent energy, and laws, and thus produces what the Hindus call "Maya," or material illusion, which they hold to be devoid of reality, inasmuch as the forms are constantly changing and have no permanence. This philosophy holds that Prakriti, by means of the glamour of its manifestations of Maya, entices the individual souls, or Purushas, which when once in the centre of attraction of the Maya are drawn into the vortex of material existence, losing a knowledge of their real nature. But the souls never lose entirely the glimmer of the Light of the Spirit, and, consequently, soon begin to feel that they have made a mistake, and consequently begin to strive to escape the bondage of Prakriti and its Maya—but such escape is possible only through a gradual rising up from the depths of Maya, step by step, cycle by cycle, by a series of purification and cleansing of themselves, just as a fly cleanses itself of the sticky substance into which it has fallen. This escape is accomplished by Spiritual Unfoldment or Evolution, by means of Reincarnation—this Evolution not being a "growth," but rather an "unfoldment" or "unwrapping" of the soul from its confining sheaths, one by one.

Another great school of Hindu philosophy is the philosophy of Patanjali, generally known as the Yoga Philosophy, but which differs from the Yogi Philosophy of the West, which is eclectic in nature. The Yoga Philosophy of Patanjali bears some resemblance to the Sankhya school of Kapila, inasmuch as it recognizes the teachings regarding Prakriti, from which universal energy the material universe has been evolved; and inasmuch as it also recognizes the countless individual Purushas, or souls, which are eternal and immortal, and which are entrapped in the Maya of Prakriti. But it then takes a position widely divergent from the Sankhya school, inasmuch as Patanjali's Yoga school holds that there also exists a Supreme

Purusha, Spirit, Soul—or God—who is without form; infinite; eternal; and above all at tributes and qualities common to man. In this respect, Patanjali differs from Kapila, and inclines rather toward agreement with Kanada, of the first mentioned school of the Vaisheshika system. All three philosophers, however, seem to generally agree in the main upon the Mind Principle, which they hold to be beneath Soul or Spirit, and to be in the nature of Mind-Stuff, which is of a semi-material nature—Kapila and Patanjali even going so far as to hold that it is a manifestation of Prakriti or the Universal Energy, rather than a distinct principle. They hold that the Purusha, or Spirit, not the Mind, is the Real Self, and the source of consciousness and the real intelligence. The practical teachings of the school of Patanjali is a system by which the Purusha may escape from and overcome the Prakriti, and thus gain emancipation, freedom, and a return to its natural and original purity and power. This school, of course, teaches Reincarnation, and Progression through Rebirth, in accordance with the principles mentioned above.

Another great school of Hindu philosophy is that known as the Vedanta Philosophy, which many consider the most advanced of all the Hindu systems, and which is rapidly growing in popularity among the educated Hindus, and also among many very intelligent students of philosophical thought in the Western world. Its followers claim that the Vedanta Philosophy has reached the very highest point of philosophical thought, speculation and analysis possible to the human mind of today, and many Western students have claimed that it contains the highest conceptions found in any and all of the great World Philosophies. Be this as it may, it certainly contains much that is the most subtle, refined and keen in the field of philosophical speculative thought of the world, and while, as some claim, it may lack the "appeal to the religious emotions" that some other forms of thought possess, still it proves very attractive to those in whom intellectual development and effort have superseded the "emotional" side of philosophy or religion.

The Vedanta System holds that the Ultimate Reality, or Actual Being, of the universe—the One Absolute Energy or Substance from which all the universe proceeds—is THAT which may be called The Absolute, which is eternal, infinite, indivisible, beyond attributes and qualities, and which is the source of intelligence. The Absolute is held to be One, not Many—Unique and Alone. It is identical with the Sanscrit "Brahman," and is held to be THAT which has been called "The Unknowable"; the "Father"; the "Over-Soul"; the "Thing-in-Itself"—in short, it is THAT which men mean, and have always meant, when they wished to express the ABSOLUTE REALITY. The Vedantists hold that this Absolute Brahman is the essence of "Sat," or Absolute Existence; "Chit," or Absolute Intelligence; and "Ananda," or Absolute Bliss. Without attempting to enter into an analysis, or close exposition, of the Vedanta Philosophy, or so far as concerns the soul, and its destiny, we may say that it holds that there do not exist the countless eter nal, immortal souls or Purushas of the Sankhya philosophy, but instead that the individual souls are but the countless "images or reflections" of the Absolute Being, or Brahman, and have their existence only by reason of the Real Existence of the One Only Being. Consequently, the Spirit within the soul of Man, and which is "the soul of his soul," is Divine. The Vedantists admit the existence of a "Logos," or Ishwara, the Lord of the Universe, who is, however, but a manifestation of Brahman—a Great Soul, as it were, and who presides over the evolution of Universes from the Prakriti, and who plays the part of the Demiurge of the old Grecian and Gnostic philosophies. The Vedantists admit the existence (relative) of Prakriti, or Universal Energy, but hold that it is not eternal, or real-in-itself, but is practically identical with Maya, and may be regarded as a form of the Creative Energy of the Absolute, Brahman. This Maya (which while strictly speaking is illusion inasmuch as it has no real existence or eternal quality) is the source of time, space, and causation, and of the phenomenal universe, with its countless forms, shapes, and appearances. The Vedantists teach that the Evolution of the Soul is accomplished by its escaping the folds of Maya, or Materiality, one by one, by means of Rebirths, until it manifests more and more of its Divine Nature; and thus it goes on, and on, from higher to still higher, until at last it enters into the Divine Being and attains Union with God, and is "One with the Father."

Another great Hindu philosophy is the philosophy of Gautama, the Buddha, which is generally known as the Buddhistic Philosophy, or as Buddhism. It is difficult to give a clear idea of Buddhism in a concise form, for there are so many schools, sects, and divisions among this general school of philosophy, differing upon the minor points and details of doctrine, that it requires a lengthy consideration in order to clear away the disputed points. Speaking generally, however, it may be said that the Buddhists start with the idea or conception of an Unknowable Reality, back of and under all forms and activity of the phenomenal universe. Buddha refused to discuss the nature of this Reality, practically holding it to be Unknowable, and in the nature of an Absolute Nothing, rather than an Absolute Something in the sense of "Thingness" as we understand the term; that is to say, it is a No-Thing, rather than a Thing—consequently it is beyond thought, understanding, or even imagination—all that can be said is that it IS. Buddha refused to discuss or teach of the manner in which this Unknowable came to manifest upon the Relative Plane, for he held that Man's proper study was of the World of Things, and how to escape therefrom. In a vague way, however, Buddhism holds that in some way this Unknowable, or a part thereof, becomes entangled in Maya or Illusion, through Avidya or Ignorance,

Law, Necessity, or perhaps something in the nature of a Mistake. And arising from this mistaken activity, all the pain and sorrow of the universe arises, for the Buddhist holds that the Universe is a "world of woe," from which the soul is trying to escape. Buddhism holds that the soul Reincarnates often, because of its desires and attractions, which if nursed and encouraged will lead it into lives without number. Consequently, to the Buddhist, Wisdom consists in acquiring a knowledge of the true state of affairs, just mentioned, and then upon that knowledge building up a new life in which desire and attraction for the material world shall be eliminated, to the end that the soul having "killed out desire" for material things—having cut off the dead branch of Illusion—is enabled to escape from Karma, and eventually be released from Rebirth, thence passing back into the great ocean of the Unknowable, or Nirvana, and ceasing to Be, so far as the phenomenal world is concerned, although of course it will exist in the Unknowable, which is Eternal. Many Western readers imagine the Buddhistic Nirvana to be an utter annihilation of existence and being, but the Hindu mind is far more subtle, and sees a vast difference between utter annihilation on the one hand, and extinction of personality on the other. That which appears Nothingness to the Western Mind, is seen as No-Thingness to the Oriental conception, and is considered more of a resumption of an original Real Existence, rather than an ending thereof.

There is a great difference between the two great schools of Buddhism, the Northern and Southern, respectively, regarding the nature of the soul. The Northern school considers the soul as an entity, differentiated from the Unknowable in some mysterious way not explained by Buddha, and yet different from the individual Purusha of the Sankhya school, before mentioned. On the contrary, the Southern school does not regard the soul as a differentiated or distinct entity, but rather as a centre of phenomenal activity saturated or charged with the results of its deeds, and that therefore the Karma, or the Essence of Deeds, may be considered as the soul itself, rather than as something pertaining to it. The Northern school holds that the soul, accompanied by its Karma, reincarnates along the same lines as those taught by all the other Hindu schools of Reincarnation and Karma. But the Southern school, on the contrary, holds that it is not the soul-entity that re-incarnates (for there is no such entity), but that instead it is the Karma, or Essence of Deeds, that reincarnates from life to life, according to its attractions, desires, and merits or demerits. In the last mentioned view of the case, the rebirth is compared to the lighting of one lamp from the flame of another, rather than in the transferring of the oil from one lamp to another. But, really, these distinctions are quite metaphysical, and when refined by analysis become hair-splitting. It is said that the two schools of Buddhism are growing nearer together, and their differences reconciled. The orthodox Hindus claim that Buddhism is on the decline in India, being largely supplanted by the various forms of the Vedanta. On the other hand, Buddhism has spread to China, Japan and other countries, where it has taken on new forms, and has grown into a religion of ritualism, creeds, and ceremonialism, with an accom panying loss of the original philosophy and a corresponding increase of detail of teaching, doctrine and disciple and general "churchiness," including a belief in several thousand different kind of hells. But even in the degenerated forms, Buddhism still holds to Reincarnation as a fundamental doctrine.

In this consideration of the philosophies of India, we do not consider it necessary to go into an explanation of the various forms of religions, or church divisions, among the Hindus. In India, Religion is an important matter, and there seems to be some form of religion adapted to each one of that country's teeming millions. From the grossest form of religious superstition, and crudest form of ceremony and worship, up to the most refined idealism and beautiful symbolisms, runs the gamut of the Hindu Religions. Many people are unable to conceive of an abstract, ideal Universal Being, such as the Brahman of the Hindu Philosophy, and consequently that Being has been personified as an An thropomorphic Deity, and human attributes bestowed upon him to suit the popular fancy. In India, as in all other countries, the priesthood have given the people that which they asked for, and the result is that many forms of churchly ceremonialism, and forms of worship, maintain which are abhorrent and repulsive to Western ideas. But we of the West are not entirely free from this fault, as one may see if he examines some of the religious conceptions and ceremonies common among ignorant people in remote parts of our land. Certain conceptions, of an anthropomorphic Deity held by some of the more ignorant people of the Western world are but little advanced beyond the idea of the Devil; and the belief in a horned, cloven-hoofed, spiked-tail, red-colored, satyr-like, leering Devil, with his Hell of Eternal Fire and Brimstone, is not so uncommon as many imagine. It has not been so long since we were taught that "one of the chief pleasures of God and his angels, and the saved souls, will be the witnessing of the tortures of the damned in Hell, from the walls of Heaven." And the ceremonies of an old-time Southern negro camp-meeting were not specially elevating or ideal.

Among the various forms of the religions of India we find some of the before mentioned forms of philosophy believed and taught among the educated people—often an eclectic policy of choosing and selecting being observed, a most liberal policy being observed, the liberty of choice and selection being freely accorded. But, there is always the belief in Reincarnation and Karma, no matter what the form of worship, or the name of the religion. There are two things that the Hindu mind always accepts as fundamental truth, needing no proof—axiomic, in fact. And these two are (1) The belief in a Soul that survives the death of the body—the Hindu mind seeming unable to differentiate between the consciousness of "I Am," and "I always Have Been, and always Shall Be"—the knowledge of the present existence being accepted as a proof of past and fu ture existence; and (2) the doctrine of Reincarnation and Karma, which are accepted as fundamental and axiomic truths beyond the need of proof, and beyond doubt—as a writer has said: "The idea of Reincarnation has become so firmly fixed and rooted in the Hindu mind as a part of belief that it amounts to the dignity and force of a moral conviction." No matter what may be the theories regarding the nature of the universe—the character of the soul—or the conception concerning Deity or the Supreme Being—you will always find the differing sects, schools, and individuals accepting Reincarnation and Karma as they accept the fact that they themselves are existent, or that twice one makes two. Hindu Philosophy cannot be divorced from Reincarnation. To the Hindu the only escape from the doctrine of Reincarnation seems to be along the road of the Materialism of the West. From the above statement we may except the Hindu Mohammedans and the native Hindu Christians, partially, although care ful observers say that even these do not escape entirely the current belief of their country, and secretly entertain a "mental reservation" in their heterodox creeds. So, you see, we are justified in considering India as the Mother Land of Reincarnation at the present time.

☯☯☯

6

The Modern West.

In the modern thought of the Western world, we find Reincarnation attracting much attention. The Western philosophies for the past hundred years have been approaching the subject with a new degree of attention and consideration, and during the past twenty years there has been a marvellous awakening of Western public interest in the doctrine. At the present time the American and European magazines contain poems and stories based upon Reincarnation, and many novels have been written around it, and plays even have been based upon the general doctrine, and have received marked attention on the part of the public. The idea seems to have caught the public fancy, and the people are eager to know more of it.

This present revival of attention has been brought about largely by the renewed interest on the part of the Western world toward the general subject of occultism, mysticism, comparative religion, oriental philosophy, etc., in their many phases and forms. The World's Parliament of Religions, held at the World's Fair in Chicago, in 1893, did much to attract the attention of the American public to the subject of the Oriental Philosophies in which Reincarnation plays such a prominent part. But, perhaps, the prime factor in this reawakened Western interest in the subject is the work and teachings of the Theosophical Society, founded by Madame Blavatsky some thirty years ago, and which has since been continued by her followers and several successors. But, whatever may be the cause, the idea of Reincarnation seems destined to play an important part in the religious and philosophical thought of the West for some time to come. Signs of it appear on every side—the subject cannot be ignored by the modern student of religion and philosophy. Whether accepted or not, it must be recognized and examined.

But the forms of the doctrine, or theory, regarding Reincarnation, vary almost as much in the Modern West as in the various Eastern countries at present, and in the past. We find all phases of the subject attracting attention and drawing followers to its support. Here we find the influence of the Hindu thought, principally through the medium or channel of Theosophy, or of the Yogi Philosophy—and there we find the influence of the Grecian or Egyptian philosophical conceptions manifesting principally through the medium of a number of occult orders and organizations, whose work is performed quietly and with little recognition on the part of the general public, the policy being to attract the "elect few" rather than the curious crowd—and again we find quite a number of persons in America and Europe, believing in Reincarnation because they are attracted by the philosophy of the Neo-Platonists, or the Gnostics of the Early Christian Church, and favoring Reincarnation as a proper part of the Christian Religion, and who while remaining in the bosom of the Church interpret the teachings by the light of the doctrine of Rebirth, as did many of the early Christians, as we have seen.

The Theosophical conception and interpretation appeals to a great number of the Western Reincarnationists, by reason of its wide circulation and dissemination, as well as by the fact that it has formulated a detailed theory and doctrine, and besides claims the benefit of authoritative instruction on the doctrine from Adepts and Masters who have passed to a higher plane of existence. We think it proper to give in some little detail an account of the general teachings of Theosophy on this point, the reader being referred to the general Theosophical literature for more extended information regarding this special teaching.

Theosophy teaches that the human soul is a composite entity, consisting of several principles, sheaths of vehicles, similar to those mentioned by us in our account of Hindu Reincarnation. The Theosophical books state these principles as follows: (1) The Body, or Rupa; (2) Vitality, or Prana-Jiva; (3) Astral Body, or Linga-Sharira; (4) Animal Soul, or Kama-Rupa; (5) Human Soul, Manas; (6) Spiritual Soul, or Buddhi; and (7) Spirit, or Atma. Of these seven principles, the last or higher Three, namely, the Atma, Buddhi, and Manas, compose the higher Trinity of the Soul—the part of man which persists; while the lower Four principles, namely, Rupa, Prana-Jiva, Linga-Sharira, and Kama-Rupa, respectively, are the lower principles, which perish after the passing out of the higher principles at death. At Death the higher principles, or Triad, lives on, while the lower principles of Quarternary dissolve and separate from each other and finally disintegrate, along the lines of a process resembling chemical action.

Theosophy teaches that there is a great stream of Egos, or Monads, which originally emanated from a Source of Being, and which are pursuing a spiral journey around a chain of seven globes, including the earth, called the Planetary Chain. The Life Wave of Monads reaches Globe A, and goes through a series of evolutionary life on it, and then passes on to Globe B, and so on until Globe G is reached, when after a continued life there the Life Wave returns to Globe A, but not in a circle, but rather in a spiral, that is, on a higher plane of activity, and the round begins once more. There are seven Races to be lived through on each globe, many incarnations in each—each Race having seven sub-races, and each sub-race having seven branches. The progress of the Life Wave is illustrated by the symbol of a seven-coil spiral, sweeping with a wider curve at each coil, each coil, however, being divided into a minor seven-coil spiral, and so on. It is taught that the human soul is now on its fourth great round-visit to the Earth, and is in about the middle of the fifth Race of that round. The total number of incarnations necessary for each round is quite large, and the teaching is that none can escape them except by special merit and development. Between each incarnation there is a period of rest in the Heaven World, or Devachan, where the soul reaps the experiences of the past life, and prepares for the next step. The period of rest varies with the degree of attainment gained by the soul, the higher the degree the longer the rest. The average time between incarnations is estimated at about fifteen hundred years. Devachan is thus a kind of temporary Heaven, from whence the soul must again pass in time for a rebirth, according to its merits or demerits. Thus, accordingly, each soul has lived in a variety of bodies, even during the present round—having successively incarnated as a savage, a barbarian, a semi-civilized man, a native of India, Egypt, Chaldea, Rome, Greece, and many other lands, in different ages, filling all kinds of positions and places in life, tasting of poverty and riches, of pleasure and pain—all ever leading toward higher things. The doctrine enunciated by Theosophy is complicated and intricate, and we can do no more than to barely mention the same at this place.

Another Western form of the Oriental Teachings, known as the "Yogi Philosophy," numbers quite a large number of earnest students in this country and in Europe, and has a large circle of influence, although it has never crystallized into an organization, the work being done quietly and the teachings spread by the sale of popular books on the subject issued at nominal prices. It is based on the Inner Teachings of the Hindu Philosophy and is Eclectic in nature, deriving its inspiration from the several great teachers, philosophies and schools, rather than implicitly following any one of them. Briefly stated this Western school of Yogi Philosophy teaches that the Universe is an emanation from, or mental creation of, the Absolute whose Creative Will flows out in an outpouring of mental energy, descending from a condition above Mind, downward through Mind, Physical Energy, and Matter, in a grand Involution or "infolding" of the divine energy into material forms and states. This Involution is followed by an Evolution, or unfoldment, the material forms advancing in the scale of evolution, accompanied by a corresponding Spiritual Evolution, or Unfoldment of the Individual Centres or Units of Being, created or emanated as above stated. The course of Evolution, or rather, that phase of it with which the present human race on earth is concerned, has now reached a point about midway in the scale of Spiritual Evolution, and the future will lead the race on, and on, to higher and still higher planes and states of being, on this earth and on other spheres, until it reaches a point incomprehensible to the mind of man of today, and then still on and on, until finally the souls will pass into the plane of the Absolute, there to exist in a state impossible of present comprehension, and transcending not only the understanding but also the imagination of the mind of man as we know him.

The Yogi Philosophy teaches that the soul will reincarnate on earth until it is fitted to pass on to higher planes of being, and that many people are now entering into a stage which will terminate the unconscious reincarnation, and which enables them to incarnate consciously in the future without loss of memory. It teaches that instead of a retributive Karma, there is a Law of Spiritual Cause and Effect, operating largely along the lines of Desire and what has been called the "Law of Attraction," by which "like attracts like," in persons, environments, conditions, etc. As we have stated, the Yogi Philosophy follows closely the lines of certain phases of the Hindu philosophies from which it is derived, it being, however, rather an "eclectic" system rather than an exact reproduction of that branch of philosophy favored by certain schools of Hindus and known by a similar name, as mentioned in our chapter on "The Hindus"—that is to say, instead of accepting the teachings of any particular Hindu school in their entirety, the Western school of the Yogi Philosophy has adopted the policy of "Eclecticism," that is, a system following the policy of selection, choosing from several sources or systems, rather than a blind following of some particular school, cult or teacher.

The Yogi Philosophy teaches that man is a seven-fold entity, consisting of the following principles, or divisions: 1. The Physical Body. 2. The Astral Body. 3. Prana, or Vital Force. 4. The Instinctive Mind. 5. The Intellect. 6. The Spiritual Mind. 7. Spirit. Of these, the first four principles belong to the lower part of the being, while the latter three are the higher principles which persist and Reincarnate. Man, however, is gradually evolving on to the plane of the Spiritual Mind, and will in time pass beyond the plane of Intellect, which he will then class along with Instinct as a lower form of mentality, he then using his Intuition habitually and ordinarily, just as the intelligent man now uses his Intellect, and the ignorant man his Instinct-Intellect, and the animal its Instinct alone. In many points the Yogi Philosophy resembles the Vedanta, and in others it agrees with Theosophy, although it departs from the latter in some of the details of doctrine regarding the process of Reincarnation, and particularly in its conception of the meaning and operation of the Law of Karma.

There are many persons in the West who hold firmly to Reincarnation, to whom the Hindu conceptions, even in the West ern form of their presentation, do not appeal, and who naturally incline toward the Greek conception and form of the doctrine. A large number of these people are generally classed among the "Spiritualists," although strictly speaking they do not fit into that classification, for they hold that the so-called "Spirit World" is not a place of permanent abode, but rather a resting place between incarnations. These people prefer the name "Spiritists," for they hold that man is essentially a spiritual being—that the Spirit is the Real Man—and that that which we call Man is but a temporary stage in the development and evolution of the individual Spirit. The Spiritists hold that the individual Spirit emanated from the Great Spirit of the Universe (called by one name or another) at some distant period in the past, and has risen to its present state of Man, through and by a series of repeated incarnations, first in the form of the lowly forms of life, and then through the higher forms of animal life, until now it has reached the stage of human life, from whence it will pass on, and on, to higher and still higher planes—to forms and states as much higher than the human state than man is above the earthworm. The Spiritists hold that man will reincarnate in earthly human bodies, only until the Spirit learns its lessons and develops sufficiently to pass on to the next plane higher. They hold that the planets and the countless fixed stars or suns, are but stages of abode for the evolving Spirit, and that beyond the Universe as we know it there are millions of others—in fact, that the number of Universes is infinite. The keynote of this doctrine may be stated as "Eternal Progression" toward the Divine Spirit. The Spirits do not insist upon any particular theory regarding the constitution of the soul—some of them speak merely of "soul and body," while others hold to the seven-fold being—the general idea being that this is unimportant, as the essential Spirit is after all the Real Self, and it matters little about the number or names of its temporary garments or vehicles of expression.

Still another class of Reincarnationists in the Western World incline rather more toward the Grecian and Egyptian forms of the doctrine, than the Hindu—the ideas of the Neo-Platonists which had such a powerful effect upon the early Christian Church, or rather among the "elect few" among the early Fathers of the Church, seeming to have sprung into renewed activity among this class. These people, as we have said in the beginning of this chapter, are rather inclined to group themselves into small organizations or secret orders, rather than to form popular cults. They follow the examples of the ancients in this respect, preferring the "few elect" to the curious general public who merely wish to "taste or nibble" at the Truth. Many of these organizations are not known to the public, as they studiously avoid publicity or advertisement, and trust to the Law of Attraction to "bring their own to them—and them to their own." The teachings of this class vary in interpretation, and as many of them maintain secrecy by pledges or oaths, it is not possible to give their teachings in detail.

But, generally speaking, they base their doctrines on the general principle that Man's present condition is due to the "Descent of Spirit," in the nature of "The Fall of Man," occurring some time in the far distant past. They hold that Man was originally "Spirit Pure and Free," from which blissful state he was enticed by the glamour of Material Life, and he accordingly fell from his higher state, lower and lower until he was sunken deep into the mire of Matter. From this lowly state he then began to work up, or evolve, having in the dim recesses of his soul a glimmer of remembrance of his former state, which dim light is constantly urging him on and on, toward his former estate, in spite of his frequent stumbling into the mire in his attempts to rise above it. This teaching holds to a theory and doctrine very similar to that of the "Spiritists" just mentioned, except that while the latter, in common with the majority of

Reincarnationists, hold that the evolution of the Soul is in the direction of advancement and greater expression, similar to the growth of a child, these "secret order" people hold forcibly and earnestly to the idea that the evolution is merely a "Returning of the Prodigal" to his "Father's Mansion"—the parable of the Prodigal Son, and that of the Expulsion from Eden, being held as veiled allegories of their teaching.

In the above view, the present state of existence—this Earthly Life—is one of a series of Hells, in the great Hell of Matter, from which Man is creeping up slowly but surely. According to this idea, the Earth is but midway in the scale, there being depths of Materiality almost impossible of belief, and on the other hand, heights of heavenly bliss equally incapable of understanding. This is about all that we can say regarding this form of the doctrine, without violating certain confidences that have been reposed in us. We fear that we have said too much as it is, but inasmuch as one would have to be able to "read between the lines" to understand fully, we trust that those who have favored us with these confidences will pardon us.

There is still another class of believers in Reincarnation, of which even the general public is not fully aware, for this class does not have much to say regarding its beliefs. I allude to those in the ranks of the orthodox Christian Church, who have outgrown the ordinary doctrines, and who, while adhering firmly to the fundamental Christian Doctrines, and while clinging closely to the Teachings of Jesus the Christ, still find in the idea of Rebirth a doctrine that appeals to their souls and minds as closer to their "highest conceptions of immortality" than the ordinary teachings of "the resurrection of the body," or the vague doctrines that are taking its place. These Christian Reincarnationists find nothing in the doctrine of Reincarnation antagonistic to their Faith, and nothing in their Faith antagonistic to the doctrine of Reincarnation. They do not use the term

Reincarnation usually, but prefer the term "Rebirth" as more closely expressing their thought; besides which the former term has a suggestion of "pagan and heathen" origin which is distasteful to them. These people are inclined toward Rebirth for the reason that it "gives the soul Another Chance to Redeem Itself"—other chances to perfect itself to enter the Heavenly Realms. They do not hold to an idea of endless reincarnation, or even of continued earthly incarnation for all, their idea being that the soul that is prepared to enter heaven passes on there at once, having learned enough and earned enough merit in the few lives it has lived on earth—while the unprepared, undeveloped, and unfit, are bound to come back and back again until they have attained Perfection sufficient to enable them to advance to the Heaven World.

A large number of the Christian Reincarnationists, if I may call them by that name, hold that Heaven is a place or state of Eternal Progression, rather than a fixed state or place—that there is no standing still in Heaven or Earth—that "In my Father's House are Many Mansions." To the majority, this idea of Progression in the Higher Planes seems to be a natural accompaniment to the Spiritual Progres sion that leads to the Higher Planes, or Heaven. At any rate, the two ideas seem always to have run together in the human mind when the general subject has been under consideration, whether in past time or present; whether among Christians or "pagans and heathen." There seems to be an intuitive recognition of the connection of the two ideas. And on the other hand, there seems to be a close connection between the several views of "special creation" of the soul before both—the single earth-life—and the eternity of reward or punishment in a state or place lacking progression or change. Human thought on the subject seems to divide itself into two distinct and opposing groups.

There are quite a number of Christian preachers, and members of orthodox churches, who are taking an earnest interest in this doctrine of Rebirth, and Eternal Progression here and hereafter. It is being considered by many whose church associates do not suspect them of being other than strictly orthodox in their views. Some day there will be a "break ing out" of this idea in the churches, when the believers in the doctrine grow in numbers and influence. It will not surprise careful observers to see the Church once more accepting the doctrine of Rebirth and reinstating the doctrine of Pre-existence—returning to two of its original truths, long since discarded by order of the Councils. Prof. Bowen has said: "It seems to me that a firm and well-grounded faith in the doctrine of Christian Metempsychosis might help to regenerate the world. For it would be a faith not hedged round with many of the difficulties and objections which beset other forms of doctrine, and it offers distinct and pungent motives for trying to lead a more Christian life, and for loving and helping our brother-man." And as James Freeman Clarke has said: "It would be curious if we should find science and philosophy taking up again the old theory of metempsychosis, remodelling it to suit our present modes of religious and scientific thought, and launching it again on the wide ocean of human belief. But stranger things have happened in the history of human opinion."

So, as we have said, there is a great variety of shades of belief in the Western world regarding Reincarnation today, and the student will have no difficulty in finding just the shade of opinion best suited to his taste, temperament and training or experience. Vary as they do in detail, and theory, there is still the same fundamental and basic truth of the One Source—the One Life—and Reincarnation, reaching ever toward perfection and divinity. It seems impossible to disguise the doctrine so as to change its basic qualities—it will always show its original shape. And, so it is with the varying opinions of the Western thought regarding it—the various cults advocating some form of its doctrine—the original doctrine may be learned and understood in spite of the fanciful dressings bestowed upon it. "The Truth is One—Men call it by many names."

It may be of interest to Western readers to mention that some of the teachers of Occultism and Reincarnation hold that the present revival of interest on the subject in the Western world is due to the fact that in Europe and America, more particularly the latter, there is occurring a reincarnating of the souls of many persons who lived from fifteen hundred to two thousand years ago, and who were then believers in the doctrine. According to this view, those who are now attracted toward the Hindu forms of the doctrine formerly lived as natives of India; those who favor the Grecian idea, lived in Ancient Greece; others favor the Egyptian idea, from similar reasons; while the revival of Neo-Platonism, Gnosticism and general Mysticism, among the present-day Christians is accounted for by the fact that the early Christians are now reincarnating in the Western world, having been reborn as Christians according to the Law of Karmic Attraction. In this manner the advocates of the doctrine offer the present revival as another proof of their teachings.

☯☯☯

~7~

Between and Beyond Incarnations.

One of the first questions usually asked by students of the subject of Reincarnation is: "Where does the soul dwell between incarnations; does it incarnate immediately after death; and what is its final abode or state?" This question, or questions, have been asked from the beginning, and probably will be asked so long as the human mind dwells upon the subject. And many are the answers that have been given to the questioners by the teachers and "authorities" upon the subject. Let us consider some of the leading and more "authoritative" answers.

In the first place, let us consider that phase of the question which asks: "Does the soul incarnate immediately after death?" Some of the earlier Reincarnationists believed and taught that the soul reincarnated shortly after death, the short period between incarnations being used by the soul in adjusting itself, striking a balance of character, and preparing for a new birth. Others held that there was a period of waiting and rest between incarnations, in which the soul 'mentally digested' the experiences of the last life just completed, and then considered and meditated over the mistakes it had made, and determined to rectify the mistakes in the next life—it being held that when the soul was relieved of the necessities of material existence, it could think more clearly of the moral nature of its acts, and would be able to realize the spiritual side of itself more distinctly, in addition to having the benefit of the spiritual perspective occasioned by its distance from the active scenes of life, and thus being able to better gauge the respective "worth-whileness" of the things of material life.

At the present time, the most advanced students of the subject hold that the average period of rest between incarnations is about fifteen hundred years, the less ad vanced souls hastening back to earth in a very short time, the more advanced preferring a long period of rest, meditation and preparation for a new life. It is held that the soul of a gross, material, animal-like person will incarnate very shortly after death, the period of rest and meditation being very short, for the reason that there is very little about which such a soul could meditate, as all of its attractions and desires are connected with material life. Many souls are so "earth-bound" that they rush back at once into material embodiment if the conditions for rebirth are favorable, and they are generally favorable for there seems to be always an abundant supply of new bodies suitable for such souls in the families of people of the same character and nature, which afford congenial opportunities for such a soul to reincarnate. Other souls which have progressed a little further along the path of attainment, have cultivated the higher part of themselves somewhat, and enjoy to a greater extent the period of meditation and spiritual life afforded them. And so, as the scale advances—as the attraction for material life grows less, the period of purely spiritual existence between incarnations grows longer, and it is said that the souls of persons who are highly developed spiritually sometimes dwell in the state of rest for ten thousand years or more, unless they voluntarily return sooner in order to take part in the work of uplifting the world. It must be remembered, in this connection, that the best teaching is to the effect that the advanced souls are rapidly unfolding into the state in which they are enabled to preserve consciousness in future births, instead of losing it as is the usual case, and thus they take a conscious part in the selection of the conditions for rebirth, which is wisely denied persons of a more material nature and less spiritual development.

The next phase of the question: "Where does the soul dwell between incarnations?" is one still more difficult of answer, owing to the various shades of opinion on the subject. Still there is a fundamental agreement between the different schools, and we shall try to give you the essence or cream of the thought on the subject. In the first place, all occultists set aside any idea of there being a "place" in which the souls dwell—the existence of "states" or "planes of existence" being deemed sufficient for the purpose. It is held that there are many planes of existence in any and every portion of space, which planes interpenetrate each other, so that entities dwelling on one plane usually are not conscious of the presence of those on another plane. Thus, an inhabitant of a high plane of being, in which the vibrations of substance are much higher than that which we occupy, would be able to pass through our material world without the slightest knowledge of its existence, just as the "X rays" pass through the most solid object, or as light passes through the air. It is held that there are many planes of existence much higher than the one we occupy, and upon which the disembodied souls dwell. There are many details regarding these planes, taught by the different schools of occultism, or spiritualism, but we have neither the time nor space to consider them at length, and must content ourselves with mentioning but a few leading or typical beliefs or teachings on the subject.

The Theosophists teach that just when the soul leaves the body, there occurs a process of psychic photography in which the past life, in all of its details, is indelibly imprinted on the inner substance of the soul, thus preserving a record independent of the brain, the latter being left behind in the physical body. Then the Astral Body, or Etheric Double, detaches itself from the body, from which the Vital Force, or Prana-Jiva also departs at the same time, the Astral Body enfolding also the four other principles, and together the Five Surviving Principles pass on to the plane of Kama Loka, or the Astral Plane of Desire. Kama Loka is that part of the Astral Plane nearest to the material plane, and is very closely connected with the latter. If the soul is filled with hot and earnest desire for earth life, it may proceed no further, but may hasten back to material embodiment, as we said a moment ago. But if the soul has higher aspirations, and has developed the higher part of itself, it presses on further, in which case the Astral Body, and the Animal Soul which is the seat of the passions and grosser desires, disintegrate, and thus release the Triad, or three-fold higher nature of the soul, namely the higher human soul, the spiritual soul, and the spirit—or as some term them, the intellect, the spiritual mind, and the spirit. The Triad then passes on to what is known as the plane of Devachan, where it rests divested of the lower parts of its nature, and in a state of bliss and in a condition in which it may make great progress by reason of meditation, reflection, etc. Kama Loka has been compared to the Purgatory of the Catholics, which it resembles in more ways than one, according to the Theosophists. Devachan is sometimes called the Heaven World by Theosophists, the word meaning "the state or plane of the gods."

Theosophy teaches that the Soul Triad dwells in Devachan "for a period propor tionate to the merit of the being," and from whence in the proper time "the being is drawn down again to be reborn in the world of mortals." The Law of Karma which rules the earth-life of man, and which regulates the details of his rebirth, is said to operate on the Devachnic Plane as well, thus deciding the time of his abode on that plane, and the time when the soul shall proceed to rebirth. The state of existence in Devachan is described at length in the Theosophical writings, but is too complex for full consideration here. Briefly stated, it may be said that it is taught that the life on Devachan is in the nature of a Dream of the Best that is In Us—that is, a condition in which the highest that is in us is given a chance for expression and growth, and development. The state of the soul in Devachan is said to be one of Bliss, the degree depending upon the degree of spiritual development of the soul, as the Bliss is of an entirely spiritual nature. It may be compared to a state of people listening to some beautiful music—the greater the musical develop ment of the person, the greater will be his degree of enjoyment. It is also taught that just as the soul leaves Devachan to be reincarnated, it is given a glimpse of its past lives, and its present character, that it may realize the Karmic relations between the cause and effect, to the end that its new life may be improved upon—then it sinks into a state of unconsciousness and passes on to rebirth.

The Western school of the Yogi Philosophy gives an idea of the state between incarnations, somewhat eclectic in its origin, agreeing with the Theosophical teaching in some respects, and differing from it in others. Let us take a hasty glance at it. In the first place it does not use the terms "Kama Loca" and "Devachan" respectively, but instead treats the whole series of planes as the great "Astral World" containing many planes, divisions, and subdivisions—many sub-planes, and divisions of the same. The teaching is that the soul passes out of the body, leaving behind its physical form, together with its Prana or Vital Energy, and taking with it the Astral Body, the Instructive Mind, and the higher principles. The "last vision" of the past life, in which the events of that life are impressed upon the soul just as it leaves the body, is held to be a fact—the soul sees the past life as a whole, and in all of its minutest details at the moment of death, and it is urged that the dying person should be left undisturbed in his last moments for this reason, and that the soul may become calm and peaceful when starting on its journey. On one of the Astral Planes the soul gradually discards its Astral Body and its Instinctive Mind, but retains its higher vehicles or sheaths. But it is taught that this discarding of the lower sheaths occurs after the soul has passed into a "soul-slumber" on a sub-plane of the Astral World, from which it awakens to find itself clothed only in its higher mental and spiritual garments of being, and free from the grosser coverings and burdens. The teachings say: "When the soul has cast off the confining sheaths, and has reached the state for which it is prepared, it passes to the plane in the As tral World for which it is fitted, and to which it is drawn by the Law of Attraction. The planes of the Astral World interpenetrate, and souls dwelling on one plane are not conscious of those dwelling on another, nor can they pass from one plane to another, with this exception—that those dwelling on a higher plane are able to see (if they so desire) the planes below them in the order of development, and are also able to visit these lower planes if they so desire. But those on the lower planes are not able to either see or visit the planes above them—not that there is a 'watchman at the gate' to prevent them, but for the same reason that a fish is not able to pass from the water to the plane of air above that water." The same teachings tell us that the souls on the higher planes often visit friends and relatives on the lower, so that there is always the opportunity for loved ones, relatives and friends meeting in this way; and also many souls on the higher planes pass to the lower planes in order to instruct and advise those dwelling on the latter, the result that in some cases there may be a progression from a lower to a higher plane of the Astral World by promotion earned by this instruction. Regarding Rebirth, from the Astral World, the teachings say:

"But sooner or later, the souls feel a desire to gain new experiences, and to manifest in earth-life some of the advancement which has come to them since 'death,' and for these reasons, and from the attraction of desires which have been smoldering there, not lived out or cast off, or, possibly influenced by the fact that some loved soul, on a lower plane, is ready to incarnate and wishing to be incarnated at the same time in order to be with it (which is also a desire) the souls fall into the current sweeping toward rebirth, and the selection of proper parents and advantageous circumstances and surrounding, and in consequence again fall into a soul-slumber, gradually, and so when their time comes they 'die' to the plane upon which they have been existing and are 'born' into a new physical life and body. A soul does not fully awaken from its sleep immediately at birth, but exists in a dream-like state during the days of infancy, its gradual awakening being evidenced by the growing intelligence of the babe, the brain of the child keeping pace with the demands made upon it. In some cases the awakening is premature, and we see cases of prodigies, child-genius, etc., but such cases are more or less abnormal, and unhealthy. Occasionally the dreaming soul in the child half-wakes, and startles us by some profound observation, or mature remark or conduct."

The third phase of the question: "What is the final state or abode of the soul?" is one that reaches to the very center or heart of philosophical and religious thought and teaching. Each philosophy and religion has its own explanation, or interpretation of the Truth, and it is not for us to attempt to select one teaching from the many in this work. The reader will find many references to these various explanations and teachings as he reads the several chapters of this book, and he may use his own discrimination and judgment in selecting that which appeals to him the most strongly. But he will notice that there is a fundamental agreement between all of the teachings and beliefs—the principle that the movement of the soul is ever upward and onward, and that there is no standing still in spiritual development and unfoldment. Whether the end—if end there be—is the reaching of a state of Bliss in the presence of the Divine One—or whether the weary soul finds rest "in the Bosom of the Father," by what has been called "Union with God"—the vital point for the evolving soul is that there is "a better day coming"—a haven of rest around the turn of the road. And whatever may be the details of the Truth, the fact remains that whatever state awaits the soul finally, it must be Good, and in accordance with Divine Wisdom and Ultimate Justice and Universal Love.

The majority of occultists look forward to an end in the sense of being absorbed in the Divine Being, not in the sense of annihilation, but in the sense of reaching a consciousness "of the Whole in the Whole" —this is the true meaning of "Nirvana." But whether this be true, or whether there is a place of final rest in the highest spiritual realms other than in the sense of absorption in the Divine, or whether there is a state of Eternal Progression from plane to plane, from realm to realm, on and on forever Godward, and more and more God-like—the End must be Good, and there is nothing to Fear, for "the Power that rules Here, rules There, and Everywhere. And remember this, ye seekers after ultimate truths—the highest authorities inform us that even the few stages or planes just ahead of us in the journey are so far beyond our present powers of conception, that they are practically unknowable to us—this being so, it will be seen that states very much nearer to us than the End must be utterly beyond the powers not only of our understanding but also of our imagination, even when strained to its utmost. This being so, why should we attempt to speculate about The End? Instead, why not say with Newman:

"I do not ask to see the distant scene.
One step enough for me –
Lead Thou me on!"

It is said that when Thoreau was dying, a friend leaned over and taking him by the hand, said: "Henry, you are so near to the border now, can you see anything on the other side?" And the dying Thoreau replied: "One world at a time, Parker!" And this seems to be the great lesson of Life—One Plane at a Time! But though the Veil of Isis is impossible of being lifted entirely, still there is a Something that enables one to see at least dimly the features of the Goddess behind the veil. And that Something is that Intelligent Faith that "knows," although it is unable to explain even to itself. And the voice of that Something Within informs him who has that Faith: All Is Well, Brother! For beyond planes, and states, and universes, and time, and space, and name, and form, and Things—there must be THAT which transcends them all, and from which they all proceed. Though we may not know what THAT is—the fact that It must exist—that It IS, is a sufficient guarantee that the LAW is in constant operation on all planes, from the lowest to the highest, and that THE COSMOS IS GOVERNED BY LAW! And this being so, not even an atom may be destroyed, nor misplaced, nor suffer Injustice; and all will attain the End rightly, and know the "Sat-chit-ananda" of the Hindus—the Being-Wisdom-Bliss Absolute that all philosophies and religions agree upon is the Final State of the Blessed. And to the occultist All are Blessed, even to the last soul in the scale of life. And over all the tumult and strife of Life there is always that Something—THAT—silently brooding, and watching, and waiting—the Life, Light, and Love of the All. Such is the message of the Illumined of all ages, races, and lands. Is it not worthy of our attention and consideration?

8

The Justice of Reincarnation.

There are three views entertained by men who believe in the existence of the soul—there are many shades of belief and opinion on the subject, but they may be divided into three classes. These three views, respectively, are as follows: (1) That the soul is specially created by the Supreme Power at the time of conception, or birth, and that its position on earth, its circumstances, its degree of intelligence, etc., are fixed arbitrarily by that power, for some inscrutable reason of its own; (2) That the soul was pre-existent, that is, that it existed before conception and birth, in some higher state not understood by us, from whence it was thrust into human form and birth, its position on earth, its circumstances, its degree of intelligence, etc., being determined by causes unknown to us; (3) That the soul is one of countless others which emanated from the Source of Being at some period in the past, and which souls were equal in power, intelligence, opportunity, etc., and which worked its way up by spiritual evolution from lowly forms of expression and life to its present state, from whence it is destined to move on and on, to higher and still higher forms and states of existence, until in the end, after millions of æons of existence in the highest planes of expressed life it will again return to the Source of Being from which it emanated, and becomes "one with the Father," not in a state of annihilated consciousness, but in a condition of universal consciousness with All. This view holds that the present condition of each soul is due to its own progress, development, advancement, unfoldment, or the lack of the same—the soul being its own Fate and Destiny—the enforcer of the Law upon itself, under the Law of Karma.

Considering the first named view, namely that the soul is newly created, and that its condition has been arbitrarily fixed by the Divine Power, the student free from prejudice or fear finds it difficult to escape the conclusion that under this plan of creation there is lacking a manifestation of Divine Justice. Even admitting the inability of the finite mind to fully grasp infinite principles, man is still forced to the realization of the manifest inequality and injustice of the relative positions of human beings on earth, providing that the same is thrust arbitrarily upon them; and it would seem that no amount of future reward could possibly equalize or explain these conditions. Unless there be "something back of it all," it would certainly seem that Injustice was manifested. Of course, many argue that the idea of Justice has nothing to do with the universal processes, but all who think of a Divine Being, filled with Love, and Justice, are compelled to think that such qualities must manifest themselves in the creations of such a Being. And, if there be nothing "back of it all," then the candid observer must confess that the scheme of Justice manifested is most faulty ac cording even to the human imperfect idea of Justice.

As Figuier, a French writer said about forty years ago: "If there are a few men well organized, of good constitution and robust health, how many are infirm, idiotic, deaf-mute, blind from birth, maimed, foolish and insane? My brother is handsome and well-shaped: I am ugly, weakly, rickety, and a hunchback. Yet we are sons of the same mother. Some are born into opulence, others into the most dreadful want. Why am I not a prince and a great lord, instead of a poor pilgrim on the earth, ungrateful and rebellious? Why was I born in Europe and at Paris, whereby civilization and art life is rendered supportable and easy, instead of seeing the light under the burning skies of the tropics, where, dressed out in a beastly muzzle, a skin black and oily, and locks of wool, I should have been exposed to the double torments of a deadly climate and a barbarous society? Why is not a wretched African negro in my place in Paris, in conditions of comfort? We have, either of us, done nothing to entitle us to our assigned places: we have invited neither this favor nor that disgrace. Why is the unequal distribution of the terrible evils that fall upon some men, and spare others? How have those deserved the partiality of fortune, who live in happy lands, while many of their brethren suffer and weep in other parts of the world?"

Figuier continues: "Some men are endowed with all benefits of mind; others, on the contrary, are devoid of intelligence, penetration and memory. They stumble at every step in their rough life-paths. Their limited intelligence and their imperfect faculties expose them to all possible mortifications and disasters. They can succeed in nothing, and Fate seems to have chosen them for the constant objects of its most deadly blows. There are beings who, from the moment of their birth to the hour of their death, utter only cries of suffering and despair. What crime have they committed? Why are they here on earth? They have not petitioned to be here; and if they could, they would have begged that this fatal cup might be taken from their lips. They are here in spite of themselves, against their will. God would be unjust and wicked if he imposed so miserable an existence upon beings who have done nothing to incur it, and have not asked for it. But God is not unjust or wicked: the opposite qualities belong to his perfect essence. Therefore the presence of man on such or such parts of the earth, and the unequal distribution of evil on our globe, must remain unexplained. If you know a doctrine, a philosophy, or a religion that solves these difficulties, I will destroy this book, and confess myself vanquished."

The orthodox theology answers Figuier's question by the argument that "in our finite understanding, we cannot pretend to understand God's plans, purposes and designs, nor to criticize his form of justice." It holds that we must look beyond that mortal life for the evidence of God's love, and not attempt to judge it according to what we see here on earth of men's miseries and inequalities. It holds that the suffering and misery come to us as an in heritance from Adam, and as a result of the sins of our first parents; but that if we are "good" it will all be evened up and recompensed in the next world. Of course the extremists who hold to Predestination have held that some were happy and some miserable, simply because God in the exercise of His will had elected and predestined them to those conditions, but it would scarcely be fair to quote this as the position of current theology, because the tendency of modern theological thought is away from that conception. We mention it merely as showing what some have thought of the subject. Others have sought refuge in the idea that we suffer for the sins of our parents, according to the old doctrine that "the sins of the parents shall be visited upon the children," but even this is not in accordance with man's highest idea of justice and love.

Passing on to the second view, namely that the soul was pre-existent, that is, existed in some higher state not understood by us, from whence it was thrust into human form, etc., we note that the questions as to the cause of inequality, misery, etc., considered a moment ago, are still actively with us—this view does not straighten out the question at all. For whether the soul was pre-existent in a higher state, or whether it was freshly created, the fact remains that as souls they must be equal in the sense of being made by the same process, and from the same material, and that up to the point of their embodiment they had not sinned or merited any reward or punishment, nor had they earned anything one way or another. And yet, according to the theory, these equally innocent and inexperienced souls are born, some being thrust into the bodies of children to be born in environments conducive to advancement, development, etc., and gifted with natural advantages, while others are thrust into bodies of children to be born into the most wretched environments and surroundings, and devoid of many natural advantages—not to speak of the crippled, deformed, and pain-ridden ones in all walks of life. There is no more explanation of the problem in this view than there was in the first mentioned one.

Passing on to the third view, namely, that the soul is one of countless others which emanated from the Source of Being æons ago, equal in power, opportunities, etc., and which individual soul has worked its way up to its present position through many rebirths and lives, in which it has gained many experiences and lessons, which determine its present condition, and which in turn will profit by the experiences and lessons of the present life by which the next stage of its life will be determined—we find what many have considered to be the only logical and possible explanation of the problem of life's inequalities, providing there is an "answer" at all, and that there is any such thing as a "soul," and a loving, just God. Figuier, the French writer, from whom we quoted that remarkable passage breathing the pessimism of the old view of life, a few moments ago, admitted that in rebirth was to be found a just explanation of the matter. He says: "If, on the contrary, we admit the plurality of human existences and reincarnation—that is, the passage of the same soul through several bodies—all this is made wonderfully clear. Our presence on such or such a part of the earth is no longer the effect of a caprice of Fate, or the result of chance; it is merely a station in the long journey that we make through the world. Before our birth, we have already lived, and this life is the sequel and result of previous ones. We have a soul that we must purify, improve and ennoble during our stay upon earth; or having already completed an imperfect and wicked life, we are compelled to begin a new one, and thus strive to rise to the level of those who have passed on to higher planes."

The advocates of Reincarnation point out that the idea of Justice is fully carried out in that view of life, inasmuch as what we are is determined by what we have been; and what we shall be is determined by what we are now; and that we are constantly urged on by the pressure of the unfolding spirit, and attracted upward by the Divine One. Under this conception there is no such thing as Chance—all is ac cording to Law. As an ancient Grecian philosopher once said: "Without the doctrine of metempsychosis, it is not possible to justify the ways of God," and many other philosophers and theologians have followed him in this thought. If we enjoy, we have earned it; if we suffer, we have earned it; in both cases through our own endeavors and efforts, and not by "chance," nor by reason of the merits or demerits of our forefathers, nor because of "predestination" nor "election" to that fate. If this be true, then one is given the understanding to stoically bear the pains and miseries of this life without cursing Fate or imputing injustice to the Divine. And likewise he is given an incentive toward making the best of his opportunities now, in order to pass on to higher and more satisfactory conditions in future lives. Reincarnationists claim that rewards and punishments are properly awarded only on the plane in which the deed, good or bad, was committed, "else their nature is changed, their effects impaired, and their collateral bearings lost." A writer on the subject has pointed out this fact in the following words:

"Physical outrage has to be checked by the infliction of physical pain, and not merely by the arousing of internal regret. Honest lives find appropriate consequence in visible honor. But one career is too short for the precise balancing of accounts, and many are needed that every good or evil done in each may be requited on the earth where it took place." In reference to this mention of rewards and penalties, we would say that very many advanced Reincarnationists do not regard the conditions of life as "rewards and punishments," but, on the contrary, look upon them as forming part of the Lessons in the Kindergarten of Life, to be learned and profited by in future lives. We shall speak of this further in our consideration of the question of "Karma"—the difference is vital, and should be closely observed in considering the subject.

Before we pass from the consideration of the question of Justice, as exemplified by Reincarnation, we would call your at tention to the difference in the views of life and its rewards and punishments held by the orthodox theologians and the Reincarnationists, respectively. On the one hand, the orthodox theologians hold that for the deeds, good or evil, performed by a man during his short lifetime of a few years, and then performed under conditions arbitrarily imposed upon him at birth by his Creator, man is rewarded or punished by an eternity of happiness or misery—heaven or hell. Perhaps the man has lived but one or two years of reasonable understanding—or full three-score and ten—and has violated certain moral, ethical or even religious laws, perhaps only to the extent of refusing to believe something that his reason absolutely refused to accept—for this he is doomed to an everlasting sojourn in a place of pain, misery or punishment, or a state equivalent thereto. Or, on the other hand, he has done the things that he ought to have done, and left undone the things that he ought not to have done—even though this doing and not-doing was made very easy for him by reason of his environment and surroundings—and to crown his beautiful life he had accepted the orthodox creeds and beliefs of his fathers, as a matter of course—then this man is rewarded by an eternity of bliss, happiness and joy—without end. Try to think of what ETERNITY means—think of the æons upon æons of time, on and on, and on, forever—and the poor sinner is suffering exquisite torture all that time, and in all time to come, without limit, respite, without mercy! And all the same time, the "good" man is enjoying his blissful state, without limit, or end, or satiety! And the time of probation, during which the two worked out their future fate, was as a grain of sand as compared with the countless universes in space in all eternity—a relation which reduces the span of man's lifetime to almost absolutely NOTHING, mathematically considered. Think of this—is this Justice?

And on the other hand, from the point of view of the Reincarnationist, is not the measure of cause and effect more equitably adjusted, even if we regard it as a matter of "reward and punishment"—a crude view by the way—when we see that every infraction of the law is followed by a corresponding effect, and an adherence to the law by a proportionate effect. Does not the "punishment fit the crime" better in this case—the rewards also. And looking at it from a reasonable point of view, devoid from theological bias, which plan seems to be the best exemplification of Justice and Natural Law, not to speak of the higher Divine Justice and Cosmic Law? Of course, we are not urging these ideas as "proofs" of Reincarnation, for strictly speaking "proof" must lie outside of speculation of "what ought to be"—proof belongs to the region of "what is" and "facts in experience." But, nevertheless, while one is considering the matter, it should be viewed from every possible aspect, in order to see "how it works out."

It is also urged along the lines of the Justice of Reincarnation, as opposed to the injustice of the contrary doctrine, that there are many cases of little infants who have only a few days, or minutes, of this life, before they pass out of the body in death. According to the anti-reincarnation doctrine, these little souls have been freshly created, and placed into physical bodies, and then without having had to taste of the experiences of life, are ushered into the higher planes, there to pass an eternal existence—while other souls have to live out their long lives of earth in order to reach the same higher states, and then, according to the prevailing doctrine, even then they may have earned eternal punishment instead of eternal bliss. According to this idea the happiest fate would be for all to die as infants (providing we were baptized, some good souls would add), and the death of an infant should be the occasion for the greatest rejoicing on the part of those who love it. But in spite of the doctrine, human nature does not so act. According to the doctrine of Reincarnation, the little babe's soul was but pursuing the same path as the rest of the race—it had its past, as well as its future, according to Law and Justice. While, if the ordinary view be correct, no one would begrudge the infant its happy fate, still one would have good cause for complaint as the Inequality and Injustice of others having to live out long lives of pain, discomfort and misery, for no cause, instead of being at once translated into a higher life as was the infant. If the ordinary view be true, then why the need of earth-life at all—why not create a soul and then place it in the heavenly realms at once; if it is possible and proper in some cases, why not in all; if the experience is not indispensable, then why impose it on certain souls, when all are freshly created and equal in merit and deserts? If earthly life has any virtue, then the infant's soul is robbed of its right. If earthly life has no virtue, the adult souls are forced to live a useless existence on earth, running the risk of damnation if they fail, while the infant souls escape this. Is this equality of opportunity and experience, or Justice? There would seem to be something wrong with either the facts, or the theory. Test the problem with the doctrine of Reincarnation, and see how it works out!

~9~

The Argument for Reincarnation.

In addition to the consideration of Justice, there are many other advantages claimed by the advocates of Reincarnation which are worthy of the careful consideration of students of the problem of the soul. We shall give to each of these principal points a brief consideration in this chapter, that you may acquaint yourself with the several points of the argument.

It is argued that the principle of analogy renders it more reasonable to believe that the present life of the soul is but one link in a great chain of existences, which chain stretches far back into the past on one side, and far out into the future on the other, than to suppose that it has been specially created for this petty term of a few years of earth life, and then projected for weal or woe into an eternity of spiritual exist ence. It is argued that the principle of Evolution on the Physical Plane points to an analogy of Evolution of the Spiritual Plane. It is reasoned that just as birth on the next plane of life follows death on the present one, so analogy would indicate that a death on past planes preceded birth on this, and so on. It is argued that every form of life that we know of has arisen from lower forms, which in turn arose from still lower forms, and so on; and that following the same analogy the soul has risen from lower to higher, and will mount on to still higher forms and planes. It is argued that "special creation" is unknown in the universe, and that it is far more reasonable to apply the principle of evolution to the soul than to consider it as an exception and violation of the universal law.

It is also claimed by some thinkers that the idea of future-existence presupposes past-existence, for everything that is "begun" must "end" some time, and therefore if we are to suppose that the soul is to continue its existence in the future, we must think of it as having an existence in the past—being eternal at both ends of the earth-life, as it were. Opponents of the idea of immortality are fond of arguing that there was no more reason for supposing that a soul would continue to exist after the death of the body, than there was for supposing that it had existed previously. A well-known man once was asked the question: "What becomes of a man's soul after death?" when he evaded the question by answering: "It goes back to where it came from." And to many this idea has seemed sufficient to make them doubt the idea of immortality. The ancient Greek philosophers felt it logically necessary for them to assert the eternal pre-existence of the soul in order to justify their claim of future existence for it. They argued that if the soul is immortal, it must have always existed, for an immortal thing could not have been created—if it was not immortal by nature, it could never be made so, and if it was immortal by nature, then it had always existed. The argument usually employed is this: A thing is either mortal or immortal, one or the other; if it is mortal it has been born and must die; if it is immortal, it cannot have been born, neither can it die; mortality means subject to life and death—immortality means immunity from both. The Greeks devoted much time and care to this argument, and attached great importance to it. They reasoned that nothing that possessed Reality could have emerged from nothingness, nor could it pass into nothingness. If it were Real it was Eternal; if it was not Eternal it was not Real, and would pass away even as it was born. They also claimed that the sense of immortality possessed by the Ego, was an indication of its having experienced life in the past, as well as anticipating life in the future—there is a sense of "oldness" pervading every thought of the soul regarding its own nature. It is claimed as an illogical assumption to hold that back of the present there extends an eternity of non-existence for the soul, while ahead of it there extends an eternity of being—it is held that it is far more logical to regard the present life as merely a single point in an eternity of existence.

It is argued, further, that Reincarnation fits in with the known scientific principle of conservation of energy—that is, that no energy is ever created or is lost, but that all energy is but a form of the universal energy, which flows on from form to form, from manifestation to manifestation, ever the same, and yet manifesting in myriad forms—never born, never dying, but always moving on, and on, and on to new manifestations. Therefore it is thought that it is reasonable to suppose that the soul follows the same law of re-embodiment, rising higher and higher, throughout time, until finally it re-enters the Universal Spirit from which it emerged, and in which it will continue to exist, as it existed before it emerged for the cycle of manifestation. It is also argued that Reincarnation brings Life within the Law of Cause and Effect, just as is everything else in the universe. The law of re-birth, according to the causes generated during past lives, would bring the existence of the soul within and in harmony with natural laws, instead of without and contrary to them.

It is further argued that the feeling of "original sin" of which so many people assert a consciousness, may be explained better by the theory of Reincarnation than by any theological doctrine. The orthodox doctrine is that "original sin" was something inherited from Adam by reason of our forefather's transgression, but this jars upon the thought of today, as well it might, for what has the "soul" to do with Adam—it did not descend from him, or from aught else but the Source of Being—there is no line of descent for souls, though there may be for bodies. What has Adam to do with your soul, if it came fresh from the mint of the Maker, pure and unsullied—how could his sin taint your new soul? Theology here asserts either arrant nonsense, or else grave injustice. But if for "Adam" we substitute our past existences and the thoughts and deeds thereof, we may understand that feeling of conscious recognition of past wrong-doing and re morse, which so many testify to, though they be reasonably free from the same in the present life. The butterfly dimly remembers its worm state, and although it now soars, it feels the slime of the mud in which it once crawled.

It is also argued that in one life the soul would fail to acquire the varied experience which is necessary to form a well rounded mentality of understanding. Dwarfed by its limited experience in the narrow sphere occupied by many human beings, it would be far from acquiring the knowledge which would seem to be necessary for a developed and advanced soul. Besides this there would be as great an inequality on the part of souls after death, as there is before death—some would pass into the future state as ignorant beings, while others would possess a full nature of understanding. As a leading authority has said: "A perfected man must have experienced every type of earthly relation and duty, every phase of desire, affection and passion, every form of temptation and every variety of conflict. No one life can possibly furnish the material for more than a minute section of such experience." Along this same line it is urged that the soul's development must come largely from contact and relationship with other souls, in a variety of phases and forms. It must experience pain and happiness, love, pity, failure, success—it must know the discipline of sympathy, toleration, patience, energy, fortitude, foresight, gratitude, pity, benevolence, and love in all of its phases. This, it is urged, is possible only through repeated incarnations, as the span of one life is too small and its limit too narrow to embrace but a small fraction of the necessary experiences of the soul on its journey toward development and attainment. One must feel the sorrows and joys of all forms of life before "understanding" may come. Narrowness, lack of tolerance, prejudice, and similar forms of undeveloped consciousness must be wiped out by the broad understanding and sympathy that come only from experience.

It is argued that only by repeated incarnations the soul is able to realize the futil ity of the search for happiness and satisfaction in material things. One, while dissatisfied and disappointed at his own condition, is apt to imagine that in some other earthly condition he would find satisfaction and happiness now denied him, and dying carries with him the subsconcious desire to enjoy those conditions, which desire attracts him back to earth-life in search of those conditions. So long as the soul desires anything that earth can offer, it is earth-bound and drawn back into the vortex. But after repeated incarnations the soul learns well its lesson that only in itself may be found happiness—and that only when it learns its real nature, source, and destiny—and then it passes on to higher planes. As an authority says: "In time, the soul sees that a spiritual being cannot be nourished on inferior food, and that any joy short of union with the Divine must be illusionary."

It is also argued that but few people, as we see them in earth-life, have realized the existence of a higher part of their being, and still fewer have asserted the supremacy of the higher, and subordinated the lower part of the self to that higher. Were they to pass on to a final state of being after death, they would carry with them all of their lower propensities and attributes, and would be utterly incapable of manifesting the spiritual part of their nature which alone would be satisfied and happy in the spiritual realms. Therefore, it needs repeated lives in order to evolve from the lower conditions and to develop and unfold the higher.

Touching upon the question of unextinguished desire, mentioned a moment ago, the following quotation from a writer on the subject, gives clearly and briefly the Reincarnationist argument regarding this point. The writer says: "Desire for other forms of earthly experience can only be extinguished by undergoing them. It is obvious that any one of us, if now translated to the unseen world, would feel regret that he had not tasted existence in some other situation or surroundings. He would wish to have known what it was to possess wealth and rank, or beauty, or to live in a different race or climate, or to see more of the world and society. No spiritual ascent could progress while earthly longings were dragging back the soul, and so it frees itself from them by successively securing them and dropping them. When the round of such knowledge has been traversed, regret for ignorance has died out." This idea of "Living-Out and Out-Living" is urged by a number of writers and thinkers on the subject. J. Wm. Lloyd says, in his "Dawn Thought," on this subject: "You rise and overcome simply by the natural process of living fully and thus outliving, as a child its milk-teeth, a serpent his slough. Living and Outliving, that expresses it. Until you have learned the one lesson fully you are never ready for a new one." The same writer, in the same book, also says: "By sin, shame, joy, virtue and sorrow, action and reaction, attraction and repulsion, the soul, like a barbed arrow, ever goes on. It cannot go back, or return through the valves of its coming. But this must not be understood to be fulfilled in one and every earth-visit. It is true only of the whole circle-voyage of the soul. In one earth-trip, one 'life,' as we say, it may be that there would nothing be but a standing still or a turning back, nothing but sin. But the whole course of all is on." But there is the danger of a misunderstanding of this doctrine, and some have misinterpreted it, and read it to advise a plunging into all kinds of sinful experience in order to "live-out and out-live," which idea is wrong, and cannot be entertained by any true student of the subjects, however much it may be used by those who wish to avail themselves of an excuse for material dissipation. Mabel Collins, in her notes to "Light on the Path," says on this subject: "Seek it by testing all experience, and remember that, when I say this, I do not say, 'Yield to the seduction of sense, in order to know it.' Before you have become an occultist, you may do this, but not afterwards. When you have chosen and entered the path, you cannot yield to these seductions without shame. Yet you can experience them without hor ror; can weigh, observe and test them, and wait with the patience of confidence for the hour when they shall affect you no longer. But do not condemn a man that yields; stretch out your hand to him as a brother pilgrim whose feet have become heavy with mire. Remember, O disciple! that great though the gulf may be between the good man and the sinner, it is greater between the good man and the man who has attained knowledge; it is immeasurable between the good man and the one on the threshold of divinity. Therefore, be wary, lest too soon you fancy yourself a thing apart from the mass." And again, the same writer says: "Before you can attain knowledge you must have passed through all places, foul and clean alike. Therefore, remember that the soiled garment you shrink from touching may have been yours yesterday, may be yours tomorrow. And if you turn with horror from it when it is flung upon your shoulders, it will cling the more closely to you. The self-righteous man makes for himself a bed of mire. Abstain because it is right to abstain, not that yourself shall be kept clean."

It is also argued that Reincarnation is necessary in order to give the evolving races a chance to perfect themselves—that is, not through their physical descendants, which would not affect the souls of those living in the bodies of the races to-day, but by perfection and growth of the souls themselves. It is pointed out that to usher a savage or barbarian to the spiritual planes after death, no matter how true to his duty and "his lights" the soul had been, would be to work an absurd translation. Such a soul would not be fitted for the higher spiritual planes, and would be most unhappy and miserable there. It will be seen that Reincarnationists make quite a distinction between "goodness" and "advancement"—while they recognize and urge the former, they regard it as only one side of the question, the other being "spiritual growth and unfoldment." It will be seen that Reincarnation provides for a Spiritual Evolution with all of its advantages, as well as a material evolution such as science holds to be correct.

Concluding this chapter, let us quote once more from the authority on the subject before mentioned, who writes anonymously in the pamphlet from which the quotation is taken. He says: "Nature does nothing by leaps. She does not, in this case, introduce into a region of spirit and spiritual life a being who has known little else than matter and material life, with small comprehension even of that. To do so would be analogous to transferring suddenly a ploughboy into a company of metaphysicians. The pursuit of any topic implies some preliminary acquaintance with its nature, aims, and mental requirements; and the more elevated the topic, the more copious the preparation for it. It is inevitable that a being who has before him an eternity of progress through zones of knowledge and spiritual experience ever nearing the Central Sun, should be fitted for it through long acquisition of the faculties which alone can deal with it. Their delicacy, their vigor, their penetrative ness, their unlikeness to those called for on the material plane, show the contrast of the earth-life to the spirit-life. And they show, too, the inconceivability of a sudden transition from one to the other, of a policy unknown in any other department of Nature's workings, of a break in the law of uplifting through Evolution. A man, before he can become a 'god,' must first become a perfect man; and he can become a perfect man neither in seventy years of life on earth, nor in any number of years of life from which human conditions are absent. * * * Re-birth and re-life must go on till their purposes are accomplished. If, indeed, we were mere victims of an evolutionary law, helpless atoms on which the machinery of Nature pitilessly played, the prospect of a succession of incarnations, no one of which gave satisfaction, might drive us to mad despair. But we have thrust on us no such cheerless exposition. We are shown that Reincarnations are the law for man, because they are the conditions of his progress, which is also a law, but he may mould them and better them and lessen them. He cannot rid himself of the machinery, but neither should wish to. Endowed with the power to guide it for the best, prompted with the motive to use that power, he may harmonize both his aspirations and his efforts with the system that expressed the infinite wisdom of the supreme, and through the journey from the temporal to the eternal tread the way with steady feet, braced with the consciousness that he is one of an innumerable multitude, and with the certainty that he and they alike, if they so will it, may attain finally to that sphere where birth and death are but memories of the past."

In this chapter we have given you a number of the arguments favorable to the doctrine of Reincarnation, from a number of sources. Some of these arguments do not specially appeal to us, personally, for the reason that they are rather more theological than scientific, but we have included them that the argument may appear as generally presented, and because we feel that in a work of this kind we must not omit an argument which is used by many of the best authorities, simply because it may not appeal to our particular temperament or habit of thought. To some, the theological argument may appeal more strongly than would the scientific, and it very properly is given here. The proper way to present any subject is to give it in its many aspects, and as it may appear from varied viewpoints.

~10~

The Proofs of Reincarnation.

To many minds the "proof" of a doctrine is its reasonableness and its adaptability as an answer to existing problems. And, accordingly, to such, the many arguments advanced in favor of the doctrine, of which we have given a few in the preceding chapters, together with the almost universal acceptance of the fundamental ideas on the part of the race, in at least some period of its development, would be considered as a very good "proof" of the doctrine, at least so far as it might be considered as the "most available working theory" of the soul's existence, past and future, and as better meeting the requirements of a doctrine or theory than any other idea advanced by metaphysical, theological, or philosophical thinkers.

But to the scientific mind, or the minds of those who demand something in the nature of actual experience of facts, no amount of reasonable abstract theorizing and speculation is acceptable even in the way of a "working hypothesis," unless based upon some tangible "facts" or knowledge gained through human experience. While people possessing such minds will usually admit freely that the doctrine of Reincarnation is more logical than the opposing theories, and that it fits better the requirements of the case, still they will maintain that all theories regarding the soul must be based upon premises that cannot be established by actual experience in human consciousness. They hold that in absence of proof in experience—actual "facts"—these premises are not established, and that all structures of reasoning based upon them must partake of their insecurity. These people are like the slangy "man from Missouri" who "wants to be shown"—nay, more, they are like the companion of the above man—the Man from Texas, who not only says: "You've got to show me," but who also demands that the thing be "placed in my hand." And, after all, one has no right to criticize these people—they are but manifesting the scientific spirit of the age which demands facts as a basis for theories, rather than theories that need facts to prove them. And, unless Reincarnation is able to satisfy the demands of this class of thinkers, the advocates of the doctrine need not complain if the scientific mind dismisses the doctrine as "not proven."

After all, the best proof along the above mentioned lines—in fact, about the only possible strict proof—is the fragmentary recollections of former lives, which many people possess at times—these recollections often flashing across the mind, bringing with it a conviction that the place or thing "has been experienced before." Nearly every person has had glimpses of something that appeared to be a recollection from the past life of the individual. We see places that we have never known, and they seem perfectly familiar; we meet strangers, and we are convinced that we have known them in the past; we read an old book and feel that we have seen it before, often so much so that we can anticipate the story or argument of the writer; we hear some strange philosophical doctrine, and we recognize it as an old friend. Many people have had this experience in the matter of Occultism—in the very matter of the doctrine of Reincarnation itself—when they first heard it, although it struck them as strange and unusual, yet they felt an inner conviction that it was an old story to them—that they "had heard it all before." These experiences are by far too common to be dismissed as mere fancy or coincidence. Nearly every living person has had some experience along this line.

A recent writer along the lines of Oriental Philosophy has said regarding this common experience of the race: "Many people have had 'peculiar experiences' that are accountable only upon the hypothesis of Metempsychosis. Who has not experienced the consciousness of having felt the thing before—having thought it some time in the dim past? Who has not witnessed new scenes that appear old, very old? Who has not met persons for the first time, whose presence awakened memories of a past lying far back in the misty ages of long ago? Who has not been seized at times with the consciousness of a mighty 'oldness' of soul? Who has not heard music, often entirely new compositions, which somehow awakened memories of similar strains, scenes, places, faces, voices, lands, associations, and events, sounding dimly on the strings of memory as the breezes of the harmony floats over them? Who has not gazed at some old painting, or piece of statuary, with the sense of having seen it all before? Who has not lived through events which brought with them a certainty of being merely a repetition of some shadowy occurrences away back in lives lived long ago? Who has not felt the influence of the mountain, the sea, the desert, coming to them when they are far from such scenes—coming so vividly as to cause the actual scene of the present to fade into comparative unreality? Who has not had these experiences?"

We have been informed by Hindus well advanced in the occult theory and practice that it is quite a common thing for people of their country to awaken to an almost complete recollection of their former lives; in some cases they have related details of former lives that have been fully verified by investigation in parts of the land very remote from their present residence. In one case, a Hindu sage related to us an instance where a poor Hindu, who had worked steadily in the village in which he had been born, without leaving it, ever since his childhood days. This man one day cried out that he had awakened to a recollection of having been a man of such and such a village, in a province hundreds of miles from his home. Some wealthy people became interested in the matter, and after having taken down his statements in writing, and after careful examination and questioning, they took him to the town in question. Upon entering the village the man seemed dazed, and cried out: "Everything is changed—it is the same and yet not the same!" Finally, however, he began to recognize some of the old landmarks of the place, and to call the places and roads by their names. Then, coming to a familiar corner, he cried: "Down there is my old home," and, rushing down the road for several hundred yards, he finally stopped before the ruins of an old cottage, and burst into tears, saying that the roof of his home had fallen in, and the walls were crumbling to pieces. Inquiry among the oldest men of the place brought to light the fact that when these aged men were boys, the house had been occupied by an old man, bearing the same name first mentioned by the Hindu as having been his own in his previous life. Other facts about the former location of places in the village were verified by the old men. Finally, while walking around the ruins, the man said: "There should be a pot of silver buried there—I hid it there when I lived here." The people rapidly uncovered the ground indicated, and brought to light an old pot containing a few pieces of silver coin of a date corresponding to the lifetime of the former occupant of the house. Our informant told us that he had personal knowledge of a number of similar cases, none of which, however, were quite as complete in detail as the one mentioned. He also informed us that he himself, and a number of his acquaintances who had attained certain degrees of occult unfoldment, were fully aware of their past lives for several incarnations back.

Another instance came under our personal observation, in which an American who had never been to India, when taken into a room in which a Hindu priest who was visiting America had erected a shrine or altar before which he performed his religious services, readily recognized the arrangement of the details of worship, ritual, ceremony, etc., and was conscious of having seen, or at least dreamed of seeing, a similar shrine at some time in the past, and as having had some connection with the same. The Hindu priest, upon hearing the American's remarks, stated that his knowledge of the details of the shrine, as then expressed, indicated a knowledge possible only to one who had served at a Hindu altar in some capacity.

We know of another case in which an acquaintance, a prominent attorney in the West, told us that when undergoing his initiation in the Masonic order he had a full recollection of having undergone the same before, and he actually anticipated each successive step. This knowledge, however, ceased after he had passed beyond the first three degrees which took him to the place where he was a full Master Mason, the higher degrees being entirely new to him, and having been apparently not experienced before. This man was not a believer in any doctrine of Reincarnation, and related the incident merely as "one of those things that no man can explain."

We know of another case, in which a student of Hindu Philosophy and Oriental Occultism found that he could anticipate each step of the teaching and doctrine, and each bit of knowledge gained by him seemed merely a recollection of something known long since. So true was this that he was able to supply the "missing links" of the teaching, where he had not access to the proper sources of information at the time, and in each case he afterward found that he had stated the same correctly. And this included many points of the Inner Teachings not generally taught to the general public, but reserved for the few. Subsequent contact with native Hindu teachers brought to light the fact that he had already unraveled many tangled skeins of doctrine deemed possible only to the "elect."

Many of these recollections of the past come as if they were memories of something experienced in dreams, but sometimes after the loose end of the thought is firmly grasped and mentally drawn out, other bits of recollection will follow. Sir Walter Scott wrote in his diary in 1828: "I was strangely haunted by what I would call the sense of pre-existence, viz., a confused idea that nothing that passed was said for the first time; that the same topics had been discussed, and the same persons had stated the same opinions on them." William Home, an English writer, was instantly converted from materialism to a belief in a spiritual existence by an incident that occurred to him in a part of London utterly strange to him. He entered a waiting room, and to his surprise everything seemed familiar to him. As he says: "I seemed to recognize every object. I said to myself, what is this? I have never been here before, and yet I have seen all this, and if so, there is a very peculiar knot in that shutter." He then crossed the room, and opened the shutter, and after examination he saw the identical peculiar knot that he had felt sure was there. Pythagoras is said to have distinctly remembered a number of his previous incarnations, and at one time pointed out a shield in a Grecian temple as having been carried by him in a previous incarnation at the siege of Troy. A well-known ancient Hindu sage is said to have transcribed a lost sacred book of doctrine from memory of its study in a previous life. Children often talk strangely of former lives, which ideas, however, are generally frightened out of them by reproof on the part of parents, and often punishment for untruthfulness and romancing. As they grow older these memories fade away.

People traveling in strange places often experience emotion when viewing some particular scene, and memory seems to painfully struggle to bring into the field of consciousness the former connection between the scene and the individual. Many persons have testified to these occurrences, many of them being matter-of-fact, unimaginative people, who had never even heard of the doctrine of Reincarnation. Charles Dickens, in one of his books of foreign travel, tells of a bridge in Italy which produced a peculiar effect upon him. He says: "If I had been murdered there in some former life, I could not have seemed to remember the place more thoroughly, or with more emphatic chilling of the blood; and the real remembrance of it acquired in that minute is so strengthened by the imaginary recollection that I hardly think I could forget it." Another recorded instance is that of a person entering a foreign library for the first time. Passing to the department of ancient books, he said that he had a dim idea that a certain rare book was to be found on such a shelf, in such a corner, describing at the same time certain peculiarities of the volume. A search failed to discover the volume in the stated place, but investigation showed that it was in another place in the library, and an old assistant stated that a generation back it had been moved from its former place (as stated by the visitor), where it had been previously located for very many years. An examination of the volume showed a perfect correspondence in every detail with the description of the strange visitor.

And so the story proceeds. Reference to the many works written on the subject of the future life of the soul will supply many more instances of the glimpses of recollection of past incarnations. But why spread these instances over more pages? The experience of other people, while of scientific interest and value as affording a basis for a theory or doctrine, will never supply the experience that the close and rigid investi gator demands. Only his own experiences will satisfy him—and perhaps not even those, for he may consider them delusions. These experiences of others have their principal value as corroborative proofs of one's own experiences, and thus serve to prove that the individual experience was not abnormal, unusual, or a delusion. To those who have not had these glimpses of recollection, the only proof that can be offered is the usual arguments in favor of the doctrine, and the account of the experiences of others—this may satisfy, and may not. But to those who have had these glimpses—particularly in a marked degree—there will come a feeling of certainty and conviction that in some cases is as real as the certainty and conviction of the present existence, and which will be proof against all argument to the contrary. To such people the knowledge of previous existences is as much a matter of consciousness as the fact of the existence of last year—yesterday—a moment ago—or even the present moment, which slips away while we attempt to consider it. And those who have this consciousness of past lives, even though the details may be vague, intuitively accept the teachings regarding the future lives of the soul. The soul that recognizes its "oldness" also feels its certainty of survival—not as a mere matter of faith, but as an item of consciousness, the boundaries of time being transcended.

But there are other arguments advanced in favor of Reincarnation, which its advocates consider so strong as to entitle them to be classed as "proofs." Among these may be mentioned the difference in tastes, talents, predispositions, etc., noticeable among children and adults, and which can scarcely be attributed to heredity. This same idea carries one to the consideration of the question of "youthful genius," "prodigies," etc.

It is a part of this argument to assume that if all souls were freshly created, by the same Creator, and from the same material, they would resemble each other very closely, and in fact would be practically identical. And, it is urged, the fact that every child is different in tastes, tempera ment, qualities, nature, etc., independent of heredity and environment, then it must follow that the difference must be sought for further back. Children of the same parents differ very materially in nature, disposition, etc.; in fact, strangers are often more alike than children of the same parents, born within a few years of each other, and reared in the same environment. Those having much experience with young babies know that each infant has its own nature and disposition, and in which it differs from every other infant, although they may be classed into groups, of course. The infant a few hours born shows a gentleness, or a lack of it—a yielding or a struggle, a disposition to adjust itself, or a stubbornness, etc. And as the child grows, these traits show more plainly, and the nature of the individual asserts itself, subject, of course, to a moulding and shaping, but always asserting its original character in some way.

Not only in the matter of disposition but in the matter of tastes, tendencies, moral inclinations, etc., do the children differ. Some like this, and dislike that, and the reverse; some are attracted toward this and repelled by that, and the reverse; some are kind while others are cruel; some manifest an innate sense of refinement, while others show coarseness and lack of delicate feeling. This among children of the same family, remember. And, when the child enters school, we find this one takes to mathematics as the duck does to water, while its brother loathes the subject; the anti-arithmetic child may excel in history or geography, or else grammar, which is the despair of others. Some are at once attracted to music, and others to drawing, while both of these branches are most distasteful to others. And it will be noticed that in the studies to which the child is attracted, it seems to learn almost without effort, as if it were merely re-learning some favorite study, momentarily forgotten. And in the case of the disliked study, every step is attended with toil. In some cases the child seems to learn every branch with the minimum effort, and with practically no effort; while in other cases the child has to plod wearily over every branch, as if breaking entirely new ground. And this continues into after life, when the adult finds this thing or that thing into which he naturally fits as if it were made for him, the knowledge concerning it coming to him like the lesson of yesterday.

We know of a case in which a man had proved a failure in everything he had undertaken up to the age of forty, when his father-in-law, in disgust, placed him at the head of an enterprise which he had had to "take over" for a bad debt. The "failure" immediately took the keenest interest in the work, and in a month knew more about it than many men who had been in the concern for years. His mind found itself perfectly at home, and he made improvement after improvement rapidly, and with uniform success. He had found his work, and in a few years stepped to the front rank in the country in that particular line of business. "Blessed is he that hath found his work." Reincarnationists would hold that that man had found his work in a line similar in its men tal demands with that of his former life or lives—not necessarily identical in details, but similar in its mental requirement. Instances of this thing are to be seen all around us. Heredity does not seem to account for it—nor does environment answer the requirements. Some other factor is there—is it Reincarnation?

Allied to this phenomena is that of "youthful genius"—in fact, genius of any age, for that matter, for genius itself seems to be out of the category of the ordinary cause of heredity and environment, and to have its roots in some deeper, richer soil. It is a well-known fact that now and then a child is born which at a very early age shows an acquaintance with certain arts, or other branches of mental work, which is usually looked for only from those of advanced years, and after years of training. In many cases these children are born of parents and grandparents deficient in the particular branches of knowledge evidenced by the child. Babes scarcely able to sit on the piano stool, or to hold the violin, have begun to play in a way that cer tainly indicated previous knowledge and technique, often composing original productions in an amazing manner. Other young children have begun to draw and design without any instruction whatever. Others have shown wonderful mathematical ability, there being several cases on record where such children have performed feats in mathematics impossible to advanced adults teaching the same lines. What are the cause of these phenomena? Is it Reincarnation?

As Figuier said, years ago: "We hear it said every day that one child has a mathematical, another a musical, another an artistic turn. In others we notice savage, violent, even criminal instincts. After the first years of life these dispositions break out. When these natural aptitudes are pushed beyond the usual limit, we find famous examples that history has cherished, and that we love to recall. There is Pascal, mastering at the age of twelve years the greater part of Plane Geometry without any instruction, and not a figment of Calculus, drawing on the floor of his chamber all the figures in the first book of Euclid, estimating accurately the mathematical relations of them all—that is, reconstructing for himself a part of descriptive Geometry; the herdsman Mangia Melo, manipulating figures, when five years old, as rapidly as a calculating machine; Mozart, executing a sonata on the pianoforte with four-years-old fingers, and composing an opera at the age of eight; Theresa Milanollo, playing the violin at four years, with such eminent skill that Baillot said she must have played it before she was born;

Rembrandt, drawing with masterly power before he could read." The same authority says, in reference to the fact that some of these prodigies do not become famous in their after years, and that their genius often seems to flicker out, leaving them as ordinary children: "That is easily understood. They come on earth with remarkable powers acquired in an anterior existence, but they have done nothing to develop their aptitudes; they have remained all their lives at the very point where they were at the moment of their birth. The real man of genius is he who cultivates and improves incessantly the great natural aptitudes that he brought into the world."

There is an interesting field for study, thought and investigation, along the lines of the early development of traits, tendencies, and thought in young children. Here evidently will be found the answer to many problems that have perplexed the race. It is true that heredity and environment plays an important part, but nevertheless, there seems to be another element working in the case, which science must have to reckon with in making up its final conclusions. Is that "something" connected with the "soul" rather than the mind of the child? Is that "something" that which men call Metempsychosis—Re-Birth—Reincarnation?

Along the same lines, or thought, lie the great questions of instinctive Like and Dislike—Loves and Hates—that we find among people meeting as strangers. From whence come those strange, unaccountable attractions and repulsions that many feel when meeting certain strangers, who could never have occasioned such feelings in the present life, and which heredity does not account for? Is it merely an absurd, irrational, fancy or feeling; is it the result of natures inharmonious and discordant; is it remnants of inherited ancestral feelings toward similar individuals hated, loved or feared; is it a telepathic sensing of certain elements in the other; or is it a manifestation of the feelings experienced in a past existence? Is this phenomena to be included in the Proofs of Reincarnation? Many people think that in Reincarnation the only answer may be found.

~II~

Arguments Against Reincarnation

The honest consideration of any subject necessitates the examination of "the other side of the case," as well as the affirmative side. We have given much space to the presentation and consideration of the arguments advanced by those convinced of the truth of Reincarnation, and before closing our work we think it well to give at least a little glimpse of "the other side" as it is presented by the opponents of the doctrine, together with the reply to the same usually made by the Reincarnationists.

The first adverse argument usually presented is that the advocates of Reincarnation have not established the existence of a "soul" which may reincarnate; nor have they proven its nature, if it does exist. The natural reply to this is that the doctrine of Reincarnation is not called upon to establish the proof of the existence of a "soul," as the idea of existence of the soul practically is universal, and, therefore, "axiomic"—that is, it is a truth that may be considered as an "axiom," or self-evident truth, worthy of being assumed as a principle, necessary to thought on the subject, a proposition which it is necessary to take for granted, an established principle of thought on the subject. Strictly speaking, perhaps the fact of the existence of the soul is incapable of material proof, except to those who accept the fact of proven "spirit return," either in the shape of unmistakable manifestation of the disincarnate soul by materialization, or by equally unmistakable manifestation in the shape of communications of some sort from such discarnate soul. Science does not admit that there are any real "proofs" of the existence of a "soul" which persists after the death of the body—but all religious, and at least the older philosophical thought, generally agrees that the existence of such a soul is a self-evident fact, needing no proofs. Many regard the statement of Descartes: "I think, therefore I am," as a logical proof of the existence of an immaterial soul, and others hold that the self-consciousness of every human being is sufficient proof that the Ego, or "I," is a something immaterial, ruling the material body which it inhabits. And so the Reincarnationists claim that this demand upon them for proof of the existence of the soul is not a fair one, because such discussion belongs to the more general field of thought; that they are justified in starting with the idea that the soul does exist, as an axiomic truth; and that their real task is to establish, not that the soul exists, but that it reincarnates after the death of the body. As Figuier says, "The difficulty is not to prove that there is a spiritual principle in us that resists death, for to question the existence of this principle we must doubt thought. The true problem is to ascertain if the spiritual and immortal principle within us is going to live again after death, in ourselves or somebody else. The question is, Will the immortal soul be born again in the same individual, physically transformed—into the same person?" As to the other objection, that the Reincarnationists have not proven the nature of the soul, to which many of the advocates of the doctrine feel it necessary to reply at great length and with much subtle reasoning, we feel that the objection is not well taken. So far as Reincarnation is concerned, if it be taken as an axiom that the soul really exists, that is sufficient as a beginning for the argument in favor of the doctrine, and the proof or disproof of any special theory regarding the nature of the soul is outside of the main question, so we shall not consider it here. It is possible to think of the soul as a reincarnating entity, whether it be a monad, duad, triad, or septenary being.

The second objection usually made is that Reincarnation cannot be true, else we would remember the incidents of our past lives, clearly and distinctly, the fact that the majority of persons have no such recollection, being held to be a disproof of the doctrine. The reply to this objection is (1) that it is not true that people do not remember the events of their past lives, the instances quoted by us, and similar ones happening to others, together with the fact that nearly every one remembers something of the past, showing that the objection is not correctly stated. And (2) that the fact that we have but a very cloudy and imperfect recollection is not an objection at all, for have we a clear recollection of the events of our infancy and childhood in this life? Have we a clear recollection of the events of twenty years ago, outside of a few scattered instances, of which the majority are only recalled when some associated fact is mentioned? Are not the great majority of the events of our present life completely forgotten? How many can recall the events of the youthful life? Old companions and friends are completely forgotten or only recalled after much thought and assistance in the way of suggested associations. Then again, do we not witness a complete forgetfulness in cases of very old people who relapse into a state of "second childhood," and who then live entirely in the present, the past having vanished for them. There are cases of people having grown old, and while retaining their reasoning faculties, were as children, so far as the past was concerned. A well-known writer, when in this state, was wont to read the books that he had written, enjoying them very much and not dreaming that he was their author. Professor

Knight says of this matter: "Memory of the details of the past is absolutely impossible.

"The power of the conservative faculty, though relatively great, is extremely limited. We forget the larger portion of experience soon after we have passed through it, and we should be able to recall the particulars of our past years, filling all the missing links of consciousness since we entered on the present life, before we were in a position to remember our ante-natal experience. Birth must necessarily be preceded by crossing the river of oblivion, while the capacity for fresh acquisition survives, and the garnered wealth of old experience determines the amount and characters of the new." Loss of memory is not loss of being—or even loss of individuality or character.

In this connection, we must mention the various instances of Double Personality, or Lost Personality, noted in the recent books on Psychology. There are a number of well authenticated cases in which people, from severe mental strain, overwork, etc., have lost the thread of Personality and forgotten even their own names and who have taken up life anew under new circumstances, which they would continue until something would occur to bring about a restoration of memory, when the past in all of its details would come back in a flash. The annals of the English Society for Psychical Research contain quite a number of such cases, which are recognized as typical. Now, would one be justified in asserting that such a person, while living in the secondary personality and consequently in entire ignorance of his past life, had really experienced no previous life? The same "I" was there—the same Ego—and yet, the personality was entirely different! Is it not perfectly fair and reasonable to consider these cases as similar to the absence of memory in cases of Reincarnation?

Let the reader lay down this book, and then endeavor to remember what happened in his twelfth year. He will not remember more than one or two, or a half dozen, events in that year—perhaps not one, in the absence of a diary, or perhaps even with the aid of one. The majority of the happenings of the three hundred and sixty-five days of that year are as a blank—as if they never had happened, so far as the memory is concerned. And yet, the same "I," or Ego, persists, and the person's character has certainly been affected and influenced by the experiences and lessons of that year. Perhaps in that year, the person may have acquired certain knowledge that he uses in his everyday life. And so, in this case, as with Reincarnation, the "essence" of the experiences are preserved, while the details are forgotten. For that is the Reincarnationist contention. As a matter of fact, advanced occultists, and other Reincarnationists, claim that nothing is really forgotten, but that every event is stored away in some of the recesses of the mind, below the level of consciousness--which idea agrees with that of modern psychologists. And Reincarnationists claim that when man unfolds sufficiently on some higher plane, he will have a full recollection of his past experiences in all of his incarnations. Some Reincarnationists claim that as the soul passes from the body all the events of that particular life pass rapidly before its mind, in review, before the waters of Lethe, or oblivion, causes forgetfulness.

Closely allied to the last mentioned argument against Reincarnation is the one that as the memory of the past life is absent, or nearly so, the new personality is practically a new soul, instead of the old one reincarnated, and that it is unreasonable and unjust to have it enjoy or suffer by reasons of its experiences and acts in the previous life. We think that the answers to the last mentioned objection are answers to this one also. The "I," Ego, or Individuality, being the same, it matters not if the details of the old Personality be forgotten. You are the same "I" that lived fifty years ago in the same body —or even ten years ago—and you are enjoying certain things, or suffering from certain things, done or left undone at the previous time, although you have forgotten the incidents. The impress of the thing is on your Character, and you are today largely what you are by reason of what you have been in past years, though those years are forgotten by you. This you will readily admit, and yet the argument of the Reincarnationists is merely an extension of the same idea. As Figuier says: "The soul, in spite of its journeys, in the midst of its incarnations and divers metamorphoses remains always identical with itself; only at each metempsychosis, each metamorphosis of the external being, improving and purifying itself, growing in power and intellectual grasp."

Another argument against Reincarnation is that it is not necessary, for the reason that Heredity accounts for all of the facts claimed as corroborative of Reincarnation. Answering this the advocates of the doctrine insist that Heredity does not account for all the facts, inasmuch as children are born with marked talents and genius, while none of their family for generations back have displayed any such tendencies. They also claim that if Heredity were the only factor in the case, there would be no advance in the races, as the children would be precisely like their ancestors, no variety or improvement being possible. But it must be remembered that Reincarnationists do not deny certain effects of Heredity, particularly along physical lines, and to an extent along mental lines, in the way of perpetuating "tendencies," which, however, are and may be overcome by the individuality of the child. Moreover, the doctrine holds that one of the laws of Rebirth is that the reincarnating soul is attracted to parents harmonious to itself, and likely to afford the environments and association desirable to the soul. So in this way the characteristics likely to be transmitted to the offspring are those which are sought for and desired by the reincarnating soul. The law of Rebirth is held to be as exact and certain as the laws of mathematics or chemistry, the parents, as well as the child, forming the combination which brings forth the rebirth. Rebirth is held to be above the mere wish of the reincarnating soul—it is in accordance with an invariable natural law, which has Justice and Advancement as its basis.

Another argument against Reincarnation is that it holds that human souls are reborn as animals, in some cases. This objection we shall not discuss, for the reason that the advanced ideas of Reincarnation expressly forbid any such interpretation, and distinctly deny its legitimate place in the doctrine. Among some of the primitive people this idea of transmigration in the bodies of animals has been held, but never among advanced occultists, or the leaders in philosophical thought favoring Reincarnation. Reincarnation teaches the Evolution of the soul from lowly forms to higher, but never the Devolution or going back into animal forms. A study of the doctrine of Reincarnation will dispel this erroneous idea from the mind of an intelligent person.

Another favorite argument is that it is repulsive to the mind and soul of the average person. Analysis of this objection will show that what is repugnant to the person is usually the fear that he will be born again without a memory of the present, which seems like a loss of the self. A moment's consideration will show that this objection is ill founded. No one objects to the idea of living in the same body for, say, ten years or twenty years more, in health. But at the end of that ten or twenty years he will be practically a different person, by reason of the new experiences he has undergone. Persons change very much in twenty years, and yet they are the same individuals—the same "I" is there with them. And at the end of the twenty years they will have forgotten the majority of the events of the present year, but they do not object to that. When one realizes that the Individual, or

"I," is the Real Self instead of the Personality, or the "John Smith, grocer, aged 36," part of them—then will they cease to fear the loss of the personality of the day or year. They will know that the "I" is the "Self"—the same yesterday, today and tomorrow. Be the doctrine of Reincarnation true or false, the fact remains that so long as YOU exist, it will be the same "I" in you that you will know that "I am." It will always be "I AM—HERE—NOW," with you, be it this moment, or a hundred years, or a million years hence. YOU can never be SOMEONE ELSE, no matter what form you wear, nor by what name you are known, nor what personality you may be acting through, nor in what place you may have your abode, nor on what plane of existence you may be. You will always be YOURSELF—and, as we have just said, it will always be "I AM—HERE—NOW" with You. The body, and even the Personality, are things akin to garments which you wear and take off without affecting your Real Self.

Then we must note another objection often made by people in discussing Reincarnation. They say, "But I do not WANT to come back!" To this the Reincarnationists answer that, if one has reached a stage in which he really has no desire for anything that the earth can offer him, then such a soul will not likely have to reincarnate again on earth, for it has passed beyond the need of earthly experiences, and has worn out its earth Karma. But they hold that but few people really have reached this stage. What one really means is that he does not want any more of Earth-life similar to that which he has been undergoing. But if he thought that he could have certain things—riches, position, fame, beauty, influence, and the rest of it, he would be perfectly willing to "come back." Or else he might be so bound by links of Karma, acting by reason of Love or Hate, Attachment or Repulsion, or by duties unperformed, or moral debts unpaid, that he might be brought back to work out the old problems until he had solved them. But even this is explained by those

Reincarnationists who hold to the idea of Desire as the great motive power of Karma, and who hold that if one has risen above all earthly desire or dislike, that soul is freed from the attraction of earth-life, and is prepared to go on higher at once, or else wait in realms of bliss until the race is ready to pass on, according to the various theories held by the various advocates of the doctrine. A little self-examination will show one whether he is free from all desire to "come back," or not. But, after all, if there is Ultimate Justice in the plan, working ever and ever for our good and advancements, as the Reincarnationists claim—then it must follow that each of us is in just the best place for his own good at the present moment, and will always be in a like advantageous position and condition. And if that be so, then there is no cause for complaint or objection on our part, and our sole concern should be in the words of the Persian sage, to "So live, that that which must come and will come, may come well," living on one day at a time, doing the best you know how, living always in the belief that "it is well with us now and evermore," and that "the Power which has us in charge Here will have us in charge There." There is a good philosophy for Living and Dying. And, this being true, though you may have to "come back," you will not have to "go back," or fall behind in the Scale of Advancement or Spiritual Evolution—for it must always be Onward and Upward on the Ladder of Life! Such is the Law!

Another objection very often urged against the doctrine of Reincarnation is that "it is un-Christian, and derived from pagan and heathen sources, and is not in accord with the highest conceptions of the immortality of the soul." Answering this objection, it may be said that, insofar as Reincarnation is not a generally accepted doctrine in the orthodox Christian Churches of today, it may be said to be non-Christian (rather than un-Christian), but when it is seen that Pre-existence and Rebirth was held as Truth by many of the Early Fathers of the Church, and that the doctrine was finally condemned by the dominant majority in Church Councils only by means of the most severe methods and the exercise of the most arbitrary authority, it may be seen that in the opinion of many of the most eminent early authorities there was nothing "un-Christian" about it, but that it was a proper doctrine of the Church. The doctrine was simply "voted down," just as were many important doctrines revered by some of the great minds of the early church, in some cases the decision being made by a majority of one vote. And, again, there have been many bright minds in the Christian Church who persisted in the belief that the doctrine was far more consistent with the Inner Teachings of Christianity than the prevailing conception, and based upon quite as good authority.

So far as the charge that it is "derived from pagan and heathen sources" is concerned, it must be answered that certainly the doctrine was accepted by the "pagan and heathen" world centuries before the dawn of Christianity, but, for that matter, so was the doctrine regarding the soul's future generally accepted by orthodox Christianity—in fact, nearly every doctrine or theory regarding the survival of the soul was "derived from pagan and heathen sources." The "pagan and heath en" mind had thought long and earnestly upon this great problem, and the field of thought had been pretty well covered before the advent of Christianity. In fact, Christianity added no new doctrine—invented no new theory—and is far from being clear and explicit in its teachings on the subject, the result being that the early Christians were divided among themselves on the matter, different sects and schools favoring different doctrines, each and all of which had been "derived from pagan and heathen sources." If all the doctrines regarding the immortality of the soul are to be judged by the test of their having been, or not been, "derived from pagan and heathen sources," then the entire body of doctrine and thought on the subject must be thrown out of the Christian mind, which must then endeavor to create or invent an entirely new doctrine which has never been thought of by a "pagan or heathen"—a very difficult task, by the way, considering the activity of the pagan and heathen mind in that respect. It must be remembered that there is no au thoritative teaching on this subject—none coming direct from Jesus. The Christian Doctrines on the subject come from the Theologians, and represent simply the views of the "majority" of some Church Council—or of the most powerful faction.

While the objection that Reincarnation "is not in accord with the highest conceptions of the immortality of the soul" is one that must depend almost entirely upon the personal bias or opinion of the individual as to what constitutes "the highest conceptions," still a comparison of the conceptions is not out of the way at this place. Do you know what was the doctrine favored by the dominant majority in the Church Councils, and for which Pre-Existence and Re-Birth finally was discarded? Do you know the dogma of the Church and the belief of masses of the orthodox Christians of the early centuries? Well, it was this: That at the death of the body, the person passes into a state of "coma," or unconsciousness, in which state he rests today, awaiting the sound of the trumpet of the great Day of Judgment, when the dead shall be raised and the righteous given eternal life IN THEIR FORMER BODIES, while the wicked in their bodies may pass into eternal torment. That is the doctrine. You doubt it? Then look over the authorities and examine even the current creeds of today, many of which state practically the same thing. This belief passed into one of the Christian Creed, in the words: "I believe in the Resurrection of the Body."

The great masses of Christians today, in general thought on the subject, speak as if the accepted doctrine of the Church was that the soul passed to Judgment, and then eternal soul life in Heaven or Hell immediately after the death of the body, thus ignoring the dogmas of the Church Councils regarding the future Day of Judgment and the Resurrection of the Body at that time. A little questioning of the religious teachers, and a little examination of religious history, and the creeds and doctrines of their respective churches, would astonish many good church members who have been fondly thinking of their beloved ones, who have passed on, as even now dwelling in Heaven as blessed angels. They would be astonished to find that the "angels" of the churches are not the souls of the good people who have been judged and awarded heavenly joys, but, rather, a body of supernatural beings who never inhabited the flesh; and that instead of their loved ones now enjoying the heavenly realms, the dogmas hold that they are now in a state of "coma" or unconsciousness, awaiting the great Day of Judgment, when their bodies will be resurrected and life everlasting given them. Those who are interested in the matter, and who may doubt the above statement, are invited to examine the records for themselves. The doctrine of the Resurrection of the Body, which is of undoubted "pagan and heathen" origin, was a favorite theological dogma of the Church in the first thousand years of its existence, and for many centuries after, and it still occupies a most important place in the church doctrines today, although it is not so often publicly preached or taught.

David Kay says: "The great distinguishing doctrine of Christianity is not the Immortality of the Soul, but the Resurrection of the Body. That the soul of man is immortal was a common belief among the Ancients, from whom it found its way at an early period into the Christian Church, but the most influential of the early Fathers were strenuously opposed to it, holding that the human soul was not essentially immortal, but only, like the body, capable of immortality." Vinet says: "The union of the soul and body appears to me essential and indissoluble. Man without a body is, in my opinion, man no longer; and God has thought and willed him embodied, and not otherwise. According to passages in the Scriptures, we can not doubt that the body, or a body, is essential to human personality and to the very idea of man."

John Milton said: "That the spirit of man should be separate from the body, so as to have a perfect and intelligent existence independent of it, is nowhere said in Scripture, and the doctrine is evidently at variance both with nature and reason." Masson, commenting on Milton's conception, says: "Milton's conception is that at the last gasp of breath the whole man dies, soul and body together, and that not until the Resurrection, when the body is revived, does the soul live again, does the man or woman live again, in any sense or way, whether for happiness or misery.... Are the souls of the millions on millions of human beings who have died since Adam, are those souls ready either with God and the angels in Heaven, or down in the diabolic world waiting to be rejoined to their bodies on the Resurrection Day? They are not, says Milton; but soul and bodies together, he says, are dead alike, sleeping alike, defunct alike, till that day comes." And many Christian theologians have held firmly to this doctrine, as may be seen by reference to any standard encyclopedia, or work on theology. Coleridge said: "Some of the most influential of the early Christian writers were materialists, not as holding the soul to be the mere result of bodily organization, but as holding the soul itself to be material—corporeal. It appears that in those days the vulgar held the soul to be incorporeal, according to the views of Plato and others, but that the orthodox Christian divines looked upon this as an impious, unscriptural opinion." Dr. R. S. Candlish said: "You live again in the body—in the very body, as to all essential properties, and to all practical intents and purposes in which you live now. I am to live not a ghost, a spectre, a spirit, I am to live then, as I live now, in the body." Dr. Arnold says: "I think that the Christian doctrine of the Resurrection meets the materialists so far as this—that it does imply that a body or an organization of some sort is necessary to the full development of man's nature."

Rev. R. J. Campbell, the eminent English clergyman, in his recent work entitled, "The New Theology," says, speaking of the popular evangelical views: "But they are even more chaotic on the subject of death and whatever follows death. It does not seem to be generally recognized that Christian thought has never been really clear concerning the Resurrection, especially in relation to future judgment. One view has been that the deceased saint lies sleeping in the grave until the archangel's trumpet shall sound and bid all mankind awake for the great assize. Anyone who reads the New Testament without prejudice will see that this was Paul's earlier view, although later on he changed it for another. There is a good deal of our current, every-day religious phaseology which presumes it still—'Father, in thy gracious keeping, leave we now thy servant sleeping.' But alongside this view, another which is a flagrant contradiction of it has come down to us, namely, that immediately after death the soul goes straight to Heaven or Hell, as the case may be, without waiting for the archangel's trumpet and the grand assize. On the whole, this is the dominant theory of the situation in the Protestant circles, and is much less reasonable than the Catholic doctrine of purgatory, however much the latter may have been abused. But under this view, what is the exact significance of the Judgment Day and the Physical Resurrection? One might think they might be accounted superfluous. What is the good of tormenting a soul in Hell for ages, and then whirling it back to the body in order to rise again and receive a solemn public condemnation? Better leave it in the Inferno and save trouble, especially as the solemn trial is meaningless, seeing that a part of the sentence has already been undergone and that there is no hope that any portion of it will ever be remitted. Truly the tender mercies with which the theologians have credited the Almighty are cruel indeed!"

But, by the irony of progress, the orthodox churches are gradually coming around to the one much-despised Platonic conception of the naturally Immortal Immaterial Soul—the "pagan and heathen" idea, so much at variance with the opposing doctrine of the Resurrection of the Body, which doctrine really did not teach the "immortality of the soul" at all. As Prof. Nathaniel Schmidt says, in an article in a standard encyclopedia: "The doctrine of the natural immortality of the human soul became so important a part of Christian thought that the resurrection naturally lost its vital significance, and it has practically held no place in the great systems of philosophy elaborated by the Christian thinkers of modern times." But still, the letter of the old doctrine persists on the books of the church and in its creeds, although opposed to the enlightened spirit now manifesting in the churches which is moving more and more toward the "pagan and heathen" conception of a naturally Immaterial and Immortal Soul, rather than in a Resurrection of the Body and an eternal life therein.

It is scarcely worth while here to contrast the two doctrines—the Immortal Immaterial Soul on the one hand, and the Immortal Body on the other. The latter conception is so primitively crude, and so foreign to modern thought, that it scarcely needs an argument against it. The thought of the necessity of the soul for a material body—the same old material body that it once cast off like a worn out garment—a body perhaps worn by disease, crippled by "accident" or "the slipping of the hand of the Potter"—a body similar to those we see around us every day—the Immortal Soul needing such a garment in order to exist! Better accept plain Materialism, and say that there is no soul and that the body perishes and all else with it, than such a gross doctrine which is simply a materialistic Immortality. So far as this doctrine being "the highest conception of the Immortality of the Soul," as contrasted with the "pagan and heathen" doctrine of Reincarnation—it is not a "conception of the Immortality of the Soul" at all, but a flat contradiction of it. It is a doctrine of the "Immortality of the Body," which bears plain marks of a very lowly "pagan and heathen" origin. And as to the "later" Christian conception, it may be seen that there is nothing in the idea of Re-birth which is inconsistent therewith—in fact, the two ideas naturally blend into each other.

In the above discussion our whole intent has been to answer the argument against Reincarnation which charges that the latter is "derived from pagan and heathen sources, and is not in accord with the highest conceptions of the immortality of the soul." And in order to do this we have found it necessary to examine the opposing theological dogmas as we find them, and to show that they do not come up to the claims of being "the highest conception," etc. We think that the strongest point against the dogmas may be found in the claims of their advocates. That the Church is now growing away from them only proves their unfitness as "the highest conception." And Reincarnationists hold that as the Church grows in favor of the Immaterial Immortal Soul, so will it find itself inclining toward the companion-doctrine of Pre-existence and Re-birth, in some of its varied forms, probably that of the Early Fathers of the Church, such as Origen and his followers—that the Church will again claim its own.

~12~

The Law of Karma.

"Karma" is a term in general use among the Hindus, and the Western believers in Reincarnation, the meaning of which is susceptible of various shades of definition and interpretation. It is most important to all students of the subject of Reincarnation, for it is the companion doctrine—the twin-truth—to the doctrine of Metempsychosis. Strictly speaking, "Karma" is the Law of Cause and Effect as applied to the life of the soul—the law whereby it reaps the results of its own sowing, or suffers the reaction from its own action. To the majority of Reincarnationists, however, it has a larger meaning, and is used in the sense of the Law of Justice, or the Law of Reward and Punishment, operating along the lines of personal experience, personal life, and personal character.

Many authorities hold that the original idea of Karma was that of a great natural law operating along exact lines, as do the laws of mathematics and chemistry, bringing forth the exact effect from every cause, and being, above all, questions of good or evil, reward or punishment, morality or immorality, etc., and acting as a great natural force above all such questions of human conduct. To those who still adhere to this conception, Karma is like the Law of Gravitation, which operates without regard to persons, morals or questions of good and evil, just as does any other great natural law. In this view the only "right" or "wrong" would be the effect of an action—that is, whether it was conducive to one's welfare and that of the race, or the reverse. In this view, if a child places its hand on a hot stove, the action is "wrong," because it brings pain and unhappiness, although the act is neither moral or immoral. And another action is "right" because it brings happiness, well-being and satisfaction, present and future, although the act was neither moral nor immoral. In this view there can be neither reward nor punishment, in the common acceptation of the term, although in another sense there is a reward for such "right" doing, and a punishment for such "wrong" doing, as the child with the burnt hand may testify to.

In this sense of the term, some of the older schools of Reincarnation accepted Karma as determining the Re-Birth, along the lines of Desire and Attraction, holding that the souls' character would attract it to re-birth along the lines of its strongest desires, and in such environment as would give it the greatest opportunity to work out those desires into action, taking the pains and pleasures of experience arising from such action, and thus moulding a new, or fuller character, which would create new Karma, which would determine the future birth, etc., and so on, and on. Those holding to this view believed that in this way the soul would learn its lesson, with many a crack over the knuckles, and with the pain of many an experience that would tend to turn it into the road most condu cive to spiritual happiness and well-being; and lead it away from the road of material desires and pleasures, because the repeated experiences had shown that no true spiritual well-being was to be obtained therefrom. In other words, the soul, in its spiritual childhood, was just like a little child in the physical world, learning by experience that some things worked for its "good" and others for "bad." This view naturally carried with it the idea that true ethics would show that whatever tended toward the advancement of the soul was "good," and whatever retarded its advancement was "bad," in spite of any arbitrary standard of right or wrong erected by man during the ages, and which standard has constantly changed from time to time, is changing now, and always will change.

But the Hindu mind, especially, soon enlarged upon this original idea of Karma, and the priests of India soon had the idea of Karma working as a great rewarder of "good," and a great punisher of "evil." Corresponding to the rewards and punish ments in the future life, as taught by Christian preachers, the Hindu priests held over the sinner the terrors of Karma; and the rewards promised the good people from the same source served to spur on the worshiper to actions in accordance with the ethics of the particular church preaching the doctrine. It was taught that the man's future state, in the next incarnation, and perhaps for many others, depended upon his state of "goodness," in accordance with the laws of the church and priestly teaching—surely as powerful an argument and as terrifying a threat as the orthodox "bribe of heaven, and threat of hell" of the Western world. The effect of this teaching is seen among the masses of the but slightly educated Hindu classes of today, who are very desirous of acquiring "merit" by performing some "good" deed, such as bestowing alms upon the wandering religious mendicant; making contributions to the temples, etc., as well as performing the acts of ordinary good will toward men; and who are as equally anxious to avoid acquiring "demerit" from the lack of prop er observances, and the performance of improper actions. While the general effect of this may be in the direction of holding the ignorant masses in the ethical road most conducive to the public weal, it also has a tendency to foster credulity, superstition and imposition, just as do similar teachings in any land, time, under the cover of any religion. There is a strong family resemblance between these teachings among all the religions, and there are many men who hold that this "crack of the theological whip" is most necessary for the keeping of the masses of the people in the strait road of morality, they being held incapable of the practice of "doing good for good's sake, and avoiding evil because it is evil." We shall not discuss this question—decide it for yourself.

One of the strongest applications of the above mentioned form of the doctrine in India is the teaching that the caste of the man in his next incarnation will be determined by his degree of "good conduct" in the present life—and that his present caste has been determined by his conduct in his previous lives. No one who has not studied the importance of "caste" in India can begin to understand how powerful a lever this teaching is upon the people of India. From the exalted Brahman caste, the priestly caste—down to the Sudra caste of unskilled laborers, or even still further down to the Pariahs or outcasts, the caste lines are strongly marked; the higher caste person deeming it the greatest disgrace to be touched by one of an inferior caste, or to eat food prepared by a lower-caste person, and so on in every act of daily life. The only comparison possible to the American mind is the attitude of the old-time Southerner toward the lowest class of negroes, and even in this case the prejudice does not extend so far as in the case of the Hindus, for the Southerner will eat food cooked by a negro servant, and will permit the latter to shave him, act as his valet, etc., something at which the high-caste Hindu would be horrified on the part of one below him in caste. This being understood, it is easy to see how careful a high-caste Hindu would be to avoid per forming actions which might rob him of his caste in his next life, and how powerful an incentive it is to a low-caste Hindu to strive for birth in a higher caste after many incarnations. To people holding such a view, birth in a low caste is the mark of crime and evil action performed in a previous life, and the low-born is accordingly felt to be worthy of no respect. We understand, from Hindu acquaintances, that this idea is gradually being dispelled in India, and an era of common human brotherhood and common interest is beginning to manifest itself.

In the Western world, the Reincarnationists, without doubt, have been greatly affected by the prevailing orthodox Hindu conception of Karma, rather than by the Grecian and general occult conception. Although there are many who regard Karma as rather a moulder of character, and consequently a prime factor in the re-birth, rather than as a dispenser of rewards and punishments—still, there are many who, discarding the orthodox Devil of their former faith, have found a worthy substi tute for him in their conception of Karma, and manifest the same terror and fear of the new devil as of the old one—and his name may be summed up as FEAR, in both cases.

Theosophists have discussed the matter of Karma very thoroughly, and their leading authorities have written much about it, its various interpretations showing in the shades of opinion among the writers. Generally speaking, however, it may be said that they have bridged over the chasm between the "natural law" idea and that of "the moral law," with its rewards and punishments, by an interpretation which places one foot on each conception, holding that there is truth in each. Of course, justice requires the reference of that student to the Theosophical writings themselves, for a detailed understanding of their views, but we feel that a brief summary of their general interpretation would be in order at this place.

One of their leading authorities states that the Law of Karma is automatic in action, and that there is no possible escape from it. He likewise holds that Absolute Justice is manifested in its operations, the idea of mercy or wrath being absent from it; and that, consequently, every debt must be paid in full, to the last penny, and that there is no vicarious atonement or exceptions made in answer to supplications to a higher source. But he particularly states that this action of the law must not be confused with ordinary reward and punishment for "good deed or bad," but that the law acts just as does any other law of Nature, just as if we put our hand in the fire we shall be burned as a natural consequence, and not as a punishment. In his statement of this view he says: "We hold that sorrow and suffering flow from sin just precisely in that way, under the direct working of natural law. It may be said, perhaps, that, obviously, the good man does not always reap his reward of good results, nor does the wicked man always suffer. Not always immediately; not always within our ken; but assuredly, eventually and inexorably." The writer then goes on to define his conception of Good and Evil. He says: "We shall see more clearly that this must be so if we define exactly what we mean by good and evil. Our religious brothers would tell us that that was good which was in accordance with God's will, and that that was evil which was in opposition to it. The scientific man would say that that was good which helped evolution, and whatever hindered it was evil. Those two men are in reality saying exactly the same thing; for God's will for man is evolution, and when that is clearly realized all conflict between religion and science is at once ended. Anything, therefore, which is against evolution of humanity as a whole is against the Divine will. We see at once that when a man struggles to gain anything for himself at the expense of others he is distinctly doing evil, and it is evil because it is against the interest of the whole. Therefore the only true gain is that which is a gain for the race as a whole, and the man who gains something without cost or wrong to anyone is raising the whole race somewhat in the process. He is moving in the direction of evolution, while the other man is moving against it."

The same writer then gives the list of the three kinds of Karma, according to the Hindu teachings, namely: "1. There is the Samchita, or 'piled up' Karma—the whole mass that still remains behind the man not yet worked out—the entire unpaid balance of the debit and credit account; 2. There is the Prarabdha, or 'beginning' Karma—the amount apportioned to the man at the commencement of each life—his destiny for that life, as it were; 3. There is the Kriomana Karma, that which we are now, by our actions in this present life, making for the future." He further states: "That second type, the Prarabdha Karma, is the only destiny which can be said to exist for man. That is what an astrologer might foretell for us—that we have apportioned to us so much good or evil fortune—so much the result of the good and evil actions of our past lives which will react on us in this. But we should remember always that this result of previous action can never com pel us to action in the present. It may put us under conditions in which it will be difficult to avoid an act, but it can never compel us to commit it. The man of ordinary development would probably yield to the circumstances and commit the act; but he may assert his free will, rise superior to the circumstances, and gain a victory and a step in evolution. So with a good action, no man is forced into that either, but an opportunity is given to him. If he takes it certain results will follow—not necessarily a happy or a wealthy life next time, but certainly a life of wider opportunity. That seems to be one of the things that are quite certain—that the man who has done well in this life has always the opportunity of doing still better in the next. This is nature's reward for good work—the opportunity to do more work. Of course, wealth is a great opportunity, so the reward often comes in that form, but the essence of the reward is the opportunity and not the pleasure which may be supposed to accompany the wealth." Another Theosophical writer says further on the subject of Kar ma: "Just as all these phases of Karma have sway over the individual man, so they similarly operate upon races, nations and families. Each race has its karma as a whole. If it be good, that race goes forward; if bad, it goes out—annihilated as a race—though the souls concerned take up their karma in other races and bodies. Nations cannot escape their national karma, and any nation that has acted in a wicked manner must suffer some day, be it soon or late." The same writer sums up the idea of individual unhappiness in any life, as follows: "(a) It is punishment for evil done in past lives; or (b) it is discipline taken up by the Ego for the purpose of eliminating defects or acquiring fortitude and sympathy. When defects are eliminated it is like removing the obstruction in an irrigating canal which then lets the water flow on. Happiness is explained in the same way—the result of prior lives of goodness."

The general idea of a number of writers on the subject of Karma is that "as ye sow, so shall ye reap," brought down to a won derful detail of arrangement, and effect flowing from causes. This conception, carried to its logical conclusion, would insist that every single bit of pain and unhappiness in this life is the result of some bad deed done either in the present life or in the past, and every bit of happiness, joy or pleasure, the result of some good action performed either in the present or past life. This conception of Karma affords us the most intricate, complex and detailed idea of reward for good, and punishment for evil (even when called "the operation of natural law") possible to the mind of man. In its entirety, and carried to its last refinement of interpretation and analysis, it has a tendency to bewilder and terrify, for the chance of escape from its entangling machinery seems so slight. But still, the same authorities inform us that every soul will surmount these obstacles, and everyone will Attain—so there is no need to be frightened, even if you accept the interpretation of doctrine in its completeness.

But there are some thinkers who carry this idea of retributive Karma to such an extreme that they hold that every instance of physical pain, disease, deformity, poverty, ill fortune, etc., that we see among people, is the inevitable result of some moral wrong or crime committed by that person in some past life, and that therefore every instance of poverty, want or physical suffering is the just result of some moral offense. Some of the extremists have gone so far as to hesitate at relieving poverty, physical pain and suffering in others, lest by so doing they might possibly be "interfering with Karma"—as if any great Law could be "interfered with." While we, generally, have refrained from insisting upon our personal preference of interpretation in this work, we cannot refrain from so doing in this instance. We consider that such an interpretation of the Law of Karma is forced and unnatural, and results from the seeming natural tendency of the human mind to build up devils for itself—and hells of one kind or another. Robbed of their Devil, many people would attribute to their God certain devilish qualities, in order that they may not be robbed of the satisfaction of smugly thinking of the "just punishment" of others. And, if they have also discarded the idea of a Personal God, their demand for a Devil causes them to attribute certain devilish qualities to Natural Law. They are bound to find their Devil somewhere—the primitive demand for the Vengeful Spirit must manifest itself in one form or another.

These people confound the action of Cause and Effect on the Material and Physical Plane, with Cause and Effect on the Spiritual Plane, whereas all true occultists teach that the Cause operating on one plane manifests effects upon the same plane. In this connection, we would call your attention to the instance in the New Testament (John IX., 2), in which Jesus was asked regarding the cause of the affliction of the man who was BORN BLIND. "And his disciples asked him, saying, 'Master, who did sin, this man, or his parents, that he was born blind?'" The question being asked in order that Jesus might determine between the two prevailing theories: (1) That the blindness was caused according to the operation of the law of Moses, which held that the sins of the parents were visited on the children unto the third and fourth generation; or (2) that it was caused according to the Law of Karma, along the lines of reincarnation, and because of some sin which the man had committed in some past incarnation (for no other interpretation of the passage is possible, and it shows the prevalence of the idea of Reincarnation among the people of that time). But Jesus promptly brushed away these two crude, primitive conceptions and interpretations, and in the light of his superior spiritual knowledge answered: "Neither hath this man sinned, nor his parents; but that the works of God should be manifest in him," the explanation of the term "the works of God" being that Jesus meant thereby the operation of the Laws of Nature imposed by God—something above punishment for "sins," and which operated according to invariable physical laws and which affected the just and the unjust alike, just as do any natural laws. It is now known that many infants are rendered blind by negligence of certain precautions at birth—this may have been a case of that kind. We consider any attempt to attribute physical infirmities to "sin" unconnected with the physical trouble to be a reversion to primitive theological dogmas, and smacking strongly of the "devil idea" of theology, of which we have spoken. And Poverty results from economic conditions, and not as punishment for "Sin." Nor is Wealth the reward of Virtue—far from it.

But before leaving this phase of the subject we would like to say that many careful thinkers have been able to discern certain spiritual benefits that have arisen from physical suffering, or poverty, and that the sufferers often manifest a high degree of spiritual development and growth, seemingly by reason of their pain. Not only this, but the divine faculties of pity, help, and true sympathy, are brought out in others, by reason thereof. We think that this view of the matter is far more along the lines of true spirituality than that of want and disease as "the punishment of sins committed in past lives." Even the human idea of Justice revolts at this kind of "punishment," and, in fact, the highest human justice and human law eliminates the idea of "punishment" altogether, so far as reprisal or revenge is concerned, the penalty being regarded merely as a deterrent of others, and a warning to the criminal against further infractions of the law, and as a reformatory agent—this at least is the theory of Human Law—no matter how imperfectly it works out in practice—and we cannot think of Divine Law being less just and equitable, less merciful and loving. The "eye for eye, tooth for tooth" conception of human justice has been out-lived by the race in its evolution.

After considering the above mentioned extreme ideas of "punishments," through the Law of Karma, we ask you to consider the following lines written by a writer having great insight, and published in a leading magazine several years ago. The idea of "The Kindergarten of God" therein expressed, we think, is far nearer in accordance with the highest Occult Teach ings, than the other idea of "Divine Wrath" and punishment for sin, along the lines of a misinterpretation of the Law of Karma, worthy of the worshipers of some ancient Devil-God. Read this little quotation carefully, and then determine which of the two views seems to fit in better with your highest spiritual conceptions:

"A boy went to school. He was very little. All that he knew he had drawn in with his mother's milk. His teacher (who was God) placed him in the lowest class, and gave him these lessons to learn: Thou shalt not kill. Thou shalt do no hurt to any living thing. Thou shalt not steal. So the man did not kill; but he was cruel, and he stole. At the end of the day (when his beard was gray—when the night was come), his teacher (who was God) said: Thou hast learned not to kill. But the other lessons thou hast not learned. Come back tomorrow.

"On the morrow he came back, a little boy. And his teacher (who was God) put him in a class a little higher, and gave him these lessons to learn: Thou shalt do no hurt to any living thing. Thou shalt not steal. Thou shalt not cheat. So the man did no hurt to any living thing; but he stole and he cheated. And at the end of the day (when his beard was gray—when the night was come), his teacher (who was God) said: Thou hast learned to be merciful. But the other lessons thou hast not learned. Come back tomorrow.

"Again, on the morrow, he came back, a little boy. And his teacher (who was God) put him in a class yet a little higher, and gave him these lessons to learn: Thou shalt not steal. Thou shalt not cheat. Thou shalt not covet. So the man did not steal; but he cheated, and he coveted. And at the end of the day (when his beard was gray—when the night was come), his teacher (who was God) said: Thou hast learned not to steal. But the other lessons thou hast not learned. Come back, my child, tomorrow.

"This is what I have read in the faces of men and women, in the book of the world, and in the scroll of the heavens, which is writ with stars."—*Berry Benson, in The Century Magazine, May, 1894.*

But there is still another view of Karma held by some Western thinkers, who received it from the Greek mystics and occultists, who in turn are thought to have received it from ancient Egypt. These people hold that the Law of Karma has naught to do with Man's theories of ethics, or religious dogmas or creeds, but has as the basis of its operations only Universal and Cosmic Principles of Action, applicable to the atom as well as Man—to the beings above Man as well. And that these universal principles of action have to do with the evolution of all things in Nature, according to well established laws. And that the evolving soul is continually striving to find the path along the lines of evolution, being urged to by the unfolding spirit within it—and that that "path" is always along the lines of least spiritual friction, and therefore along the lines of the least ultimate spiritual pain. And that, accordingly, Spiritual Pain is an indication to the evolving thing that it is on the wrong path, and that it must find a better way onward—which message it heeds by reason of the pain, and accordingly seeks out for itself a better way, and one that will bring less spiritual pain and greater ultimate spiritual satisfaction.

This teaching holds that all material things are a source of more or less pain to the growing and evolving soul, which tends to urge it along the line of the least spiritual resistence—the least spiritual friction. It may be that the soul does not recognize the direction of the urge, and insist in tasting this material pleasure (so-thought) and then that—only to find that neither satisfy—that both are Dead Sea Fruit—that both have the thorn attached to the flower—that all bring pain, satiety and disgust—the consequence being that the tired and wearied soul, when rested by the Lethal slumber, and then re-born has a horror and distaste for the things which disgusted it in its previous life, and is therefore urged toward opposite things. If the soul has not been satiated—has not yet been pricked by the hidden thorn—it wishes to go on further in the dream of material pleasure, and so it does, until it learns its lesson. Finally, perceiving the folly and worthlessness of materiality, it emerges from its cocoon and, spreading out its newly found wings, takes its flight for higher planes of action and being—and so on, and on, and on, forever.

Under this view people are not punished "for" their sins, but "by" them—and "Sin" is seen to be merely a "mistake," not a crime. And Pain arises not as a punishment for something done wrongly, but as a warning sign of "hands off"; and consequently Pain is something by which we may mount to higher things—to

Something Better—and not a punishment. And this idea holds, also, that on the physical plane physical law governs, and physical effects follow physical causes; likewise on the mental plane; likewise on the Spiritual Plane. And, therefore, it is absurd to suppose that one suffers physical pain as a punishment for some moral offense committed on another plane. On the contrary, however, this idea holds that from the physical pain which was occasioned by the operation of physical law alone one may develop higher spiritual states by reason of a better understanding of the nature of pain in oneself and others. And this idea refuses to recognize material pleasures or profits as a reward for spiritual or moral actions.

On the whole this last mentioned conception of Karma refuses to use the terms "reward and punishment," or even to entertain those ideas, but instead sees in everything the working out of a great Cosmic Plan whereby everything rises from lower to higher, and still higher. To it Karma is but one phase of the great LAW operating in all planes and forms of Life and the Universe. To it the idea that "THE UNIVERSE IS GOVERNED BY LAW" is an axiom. And while to it ULTIMATE JUSTICE is also axiomic, it sees not in the operation of penalties and reward—merits and demerits—the proof of that Ultimate Justice; it looks for it and finds it in the conception and realizing that ALL WORKS FOR GOOD—that Everything is tending upward—that everything is justified and just, because the END is ABSOLUTE GOOD, and that every tiny working of the great cosmic machinery is turning in the right direction and to that end. Consequently, each of us is just where he should be at the present time—and our condition is exactly the very best to bring us to that Divine Consummation and End. And to such thinkers, indeed, there is no Devil but Fear and Unfaith, and all other devils are illusions, whether they be called Beelzebub, Mortal-Mind, or Karma, if they produce Fear and Unfaith in the All-

Good. And such thinkers feel that the way to live according to the Higher Light, and without fear of a Malevolent Karma, is to feel one's relationship with the Universal Good, and then to "Live One Day at a time—Doing the Best you Know How—and Be Kind"—knowing that in the All-Good you live and move and have your being, and that outside of that All-Good you cannot stray, for there is no outside—knowing that THAT which brought you Here will be with you There—that Death is but a phase of Life—and above all that THERE IS NOTHING TO BE AFRAID OF—and that ALL IS WELL with God; with the Universe; and with YOU!

☯☯☯☯☯